THE WAY OF THE MINDFUL WARRIOR

THE WAY OF THE MINDFUL WARRIOR

Embrace Authentic Mindfulness for Wellbeing, Wisdom, and Awareness

William Van Gordon
and Edo Shonin

ROWMAN & LITTLEFIELD
Lanham • Boulder • New York • London

Published by Rowman & Littlefield
An imprint of The Rowman & Littlefield Publishing Group, Inc.
4501 Forbes Boulevard, Suite 200, Lanham, Maryland 20706
www.rowman.com

6 Tinworth Street, London SE11 5AL, United Kingdom

British Library Cataloguing in Publication Information Available

Library of Congress Cataloging-in-Publication Data Available

ISBN 978-1-5381-4671-2 (cloth)
ISBN 978-1-5381-4672-9 (electronic)

To my spiritual forefather—may your blessings continue to flow

W.V.G.

To the indestructible path of the Mindful Warrior, that reveals itself to all genuine seekers of the way

E.S.

When he knew that the householder Upāli's mind was ready, receptive, free from hindrances, elated and confident, he expounded to him the teaching special to the Buddhas: suffering, its origin, its cessation and the path. Just as a clean cloth with all marks removed would take dye evenly, so too, while the householder Upāli sat there, the spotless immaculate vision of the Dhamma arose in him: "All that is subject to arising is subject to cessation." Then the householder Upāli saw the Dhamma, fathomed the Dhamma; he crossed beyond doubt, did away with perplexity, gained intrepidity, and became independent of others in the Teacher's dispensation. Then he said to the Blessed One: "Now, venerable sir, we must go. We are busy and have much to do."

The Upāli Sutta, translated by Ñanamoli
and Bodhi

CONTENTS

ACKNOWLEDGMENTS

We would like to express gratitude for the various people and conditions that have made possible the writing and publication of this book. First, we would like to thank the numerous favorable and adverse situations that we have encountered during our lives. These situations have been our teachers and have allowed us to grow in patience, humility, and spiritual awareness. We would also like to thank the Buddhist and non-Buddhist teachers who have offered, and continue to offer, their support and teachings. Likewise, we would like to thank our students, friends, and family members for their patience and understanding during the times we were engaged with writing, and for their helpful feedback on numerous chapters of this book. Finally, we would like to acknowledge the help and support provided by our agent Giles Anderson of Anderson Literary Agency, as well as by the team at Rowman & Littlefield.

INTRODUCTION

Are you fully aware that you are breathing? Are you fully aware that you are alive? Are you fully present for each and every moment of your life? Or are you continuously pulled from one situation to the next, exhausted and unable to sit in stillness with yourself?

We experience every moment of our lives for the first and last time. A situation never repeats itself. It might not seem this way but the truth is that every instant of our lives is completely fresh and original. We may think we are the same person that we were last year, or we may even think that things have not changed since yesterday. But they most certainly have. Everything is in a constant state of flux. Everything changes all of the time. Each breath we take and everything we see, hear, smell, taste, and touch is 100 percent unique. Absolutely nothing stands still.

Unfortunately, although most people understand that all things are impermanent, they tend to get stuck in certain ways of seeing things and in certain ways of being. Indeed, people easily fall into the trap of believing their situation is fixed and unworkable, like a slab of solid ice that is totally unyielding. Consequently, instead of being awake to the dance of impermanence—the natural and transient state of everything—we develop a limited view of ourselves and we start to take things for granted. We tend to forget that we are only on this earth for a finite period of time, and we become blind to the wonders of life that are continuously happening all around us.

In fact, if we are being truthful with ourselves, then we probably have to admit that many people, particularly in today's fast-paced consumer society, have become experts at making soap operas out of their lives. The problem with living a soap opera is that the mind starts to close in on itself, and we become obsessed with our and others' affairs. Living a soap opera means that rather than being in the driver's seat, we are controlled almost entirely by our thoughts and emotions as well as by the thoughts and emotions of others. We get lost in the situation and this stops us from stepping back and seeing the bigger picture. If we get stuck living a soap opera, we become increasingly lost as each day goes by and our life becomes less meaningful. At first, there is a voice inside us that tells us we are missing the point and that we are starving and imprisoning that part of us that wants to be truly free. However, the more time we spend living a soap opera, the quieter and quieter the voice becomes. Eventually, we stop hearing it altogether and we begin to feel lost and exhausted, like a horse that has been captured from the wild and is worked to the breaking point.

In the midst of soap opera living, the mind is never truly satisfied. It constantly searches for temporary relief and looks for quick-fix solutions that will end its suffering. Examples of such quick-fix strategies might be diving head-first into the latest health trend, going on shopping sprees, jumping into and out of relationships, going on a spiritual trip, or turning to alcohol or drugs. However, rather than acting as a permanent solution to our dissatisfaction, these behaviors generally tend to keep us distracted in order to avoid having to confront our problems at their source.

The truth is, if we really want to break free of soap opera living, if we really want to take back control of our lives and find lasting peace and happiness, then we have to start with our current situation. We have to take ourselves exactly as we are. We have to avoid the trap of kidding ourselves that there is a quick-fix to our predicament. We have to accept that lasting change is going to take time, joyful perseverance, and warrior-like courage. As soon as we embrace these principles and accept our dilemma for what it is, our situation immediately becomes lighter. We are no longer pulling the wool over our own eyes and, at long last, we are being completely truthful with ourselves. Now we can breathe a short sigh of relief.

Soap opera living tends to make us forget who we really are and what is important in life. Therefore, if we are going to accept and work with our current situation, the first thing we must do is start to become aware of exactly who we are. Most people have difficulty admitting that they don't really know themselves, and this is why taking responsibility for our own happiness takes courage. However, if we can let go of the ego and be truthful with ourselves about this matter, then that slab of solid ice that we referred to earlier begins to melt a little—our situation no longer feels quite so cold or unworkable.

So how do we become aware of who we are? How do we start to know ourselves? The answer to these questions is quite simple—we start to observe ourselves. This is basically what is meant by the term *mindfulness*. The essence of being mindful is simply observing and being present with ourselves. Ordinarily, people are not aware of their thoughts, words, or actions. The body might be walking in the park with a loved one, but the mind is somewhere else. It is either distracted with thoughts about the future, or is preoccupied with the past. Only very rarely does one come across a person whose body and mind are fully synchronized, a person who is fully conscious of each and every breath and who is aware of every footstep that they take.

After decades of practicing and teaching mindfulness as Buddhist practitioners, and through our research as scientists and psychologists, time and time again we have witnessed people take mindful living to heart and begin to flourish as human beings. It doesn't matter where you find yourself now, every situation, without exception, provides us with possibilities to transform suffering and to grow as human beings.

Traditional Buddhist teachings use the analogy of the lotus flower to explain this principle. Even in the darkest and murkiest of water, the lotus seed is able to sprout and grow out of the mud. It gradually makes its way toward the brighter and clearer water that stands above it. When the shoot reaches a certain stage of growth, it will stop just short of breaking the water's surface. Here it will wait patiently for all the right conditions before it surfaces and blossoms into the most beautiful and vibrant of flowers.

Beautiful things can be born in the strangest and darkest of places. By slightly changing our perspective, what we think is a very difficult period in our life could become an opportunity for fostering happiness and for tapping into an inner reserve of strength, calm, and insight. A person might be going through a very distressing phase, or they might already be on the path to cultivating psychological and spiritual wellbeing—either way, practicing mindful awareness is a tried and tested means of trans-forming suffering into freedom and happiness.

The important thing to bear in mind is that practicing mindful-ness is not about reaching a goal or attaining a special state of realization or enlightenment. In fact, the opposite is true. Mind-fulness is about learning to understand that everything we need is already present, right here and right now. It is because we have a tendency to be trapped by our thoughts and drawn into fantasizing about the future or reminiscing about the past, that we never give the mind the opportunity to calm, find its bearings, and take joy in the simple fact that we are alive and breathing. However, if we make our home in the present moment, then no matter where we find ourselves, we can never be lost.

At the moment, there is a lot of interest in mindfulness from the general public as well as from scientists, corporations, and health care professionals. Indeed, a large number of books and academic papers have been written that offer various interpreta-tions of how to practice mindfulness effectively, or how to use mindfulness to cope with the stresses and strains of contemporary living. However, such texts often present mindfulness in a way that is either far removed from the traditional spiritual context of mindfulness practice, or that offers an overly technical perspective. To be blunt, there is a lot of nonsense being written about mindfulness, and there are a lot of people trying to make money or a career out of setting themselves up as mindfulness or Buddhist teachers. Therefore, in the writing of this book, we have attempted to offer a perspective that is fresh and authentic, that cuts through the hype surrounding mindfulness, and that carefully blends together the traditional Buddhist teachings with emerging insights from the use and scientific study of mindfulness in research and applied settings.

We have done this by presenting the way of life of the Mindful Warrior. Mindful Warriors are persons who, when modern society seems to want to draw them into living an ever more superficial soap opera, have the courage to stand on their own feet and embrace their innermost nature of peace, wisdom, and compassion. We are certainly not offering a quick-fix solution to overcoming suffering and life's problems, nor are we going to try to convince you to take on board the principles outlined in this text. That is a choice that you must make on your own. However, what we do offer is a structured path and philosophy, that when practiced as a way of life, can help you to find stillness and unconditional wellbeing. We have endeavored to use this book to portray the essence not just of mindful living, but of Buddhist and spiritual practice more generally. Consequently, readers are encouraged to reread the text from time to time, in order to extract new meaning as they find themselves at different stages of this journey. To the best of our ability, we have attempted to write each word of this book using mindfulness and insight. Therefore, if you decide to read on, and if you decide to walk the path of the Mindful Warrior, hopefully you will feel that we are not too far away, and that we are gently walking along the path with you.

William Van Gordon and Edo Shonin
February, 2020

I

ALLOWING THE MIND TO BREATHE

The overwhelming majority of people have very busy minds. This is different from saying that we are always very busy, because, often when we are doing very little, the mind is still working very hard. Even when we sit down to rest or go to sleep, the mind keeps on churning out thoughts, feelings, and mental chatter. In fact, wherever we find ourselves, the mind is generally absorbed in some kind of activity such as reading, writing, chatting, or otherwise entertaining itself. And for those occasions when we find ourselves with nothing in particular to do, there are various tactics that we use in order to keep boredom at bay. For example, if we are stuck in traffic on the motorway or traveling alone on an airplane or train, we will often occupy ourselves by reminiscing about the past, planning out the future, or living out some other kind of mental drama. Regardless of whether we are engaging in an activity involving another object or person, or whether we are playing out a fantasy in our minds, there is invariably another layer of background thought occurring that has nothing to do with the particular task, person, or situation in front of us.

In effect, we allow our mind to do whatever it wants, whenever it wants. We give little thought to the type of mind that we are cultivating, and whether our "mental conduct" will be beneficial or harmful to our long-term wellbeing or the wellbeing of others.

There is a saying that "you become what you think." However, traditional Buddhist teachings, and certain cognitive behavioral psychotherapeutic approaches, suggest that "you become *how* you think." In other words, our psychological wellbeing has less to do with the specific content of our thoughts or mental chatter, and more to do with whether we are aware of what we are thinking and whether we allow the mind to be easily distracted.

According to the UK's Mental Health Foundation, 25 percent of adults experience a mental health problem during the course of one year. Many psychologists—including ourselves—attribute these alarming figures to people developing maladaptive cognitive and behavioral processes. This basically means that people fall into bad thinking habits and behave in a way that is not conducive to happiness and wellbeing. Indeed, while people often go to great lengths to groom the body in order to make it attractive, very few make the same effort when it comes to grooming the mind.

This is how one office manager described the effects of neglecting the mind when she was interviewed during one of our research projects:

> Here in the West, people think that if you've been through the education system then that's your mental development complete. That's you set up for the rest of your life. But so much is left untouched. Nobody takes the time to show you how to truly care for the mind, how to stop yourself becoming stressed and worn out, or how to stop the mind from suffocating or racing away with itself. It's like we prefer people to be intelligent rather than decent and rounded human beings. But being intelligent doesn't stop you from becoming unhappy, or it doesn't stop you becoming a pig in the way you treat others. [1]

LETTING THE MIND BREATHE

Given the mind's tendency to act like a headless chicken and jump between one mental drama and another, how do we begin to slow the mind down and become less erratic in our thought processes? One way to do this is to introduce and make use of what is termed a "meditative anchor." Probably the most popular meditative anchor used in both the traditional meditation teachings and modern-day clinical mindfulness interventions is "breath awareness." Becoming aware of and following the breath helps to slow down and "anchor" the mind so that it becomes difficult for us to be distracted or carried away by our thoughts and feelings.

Unruly minds and faulty thinking patterns tend to prevent us from settling our awareness in the present moment. The reason we want to try to remain aware of the present moment is because, really and truly, this is the only place where we can fully experience life. The future will never materialize, and so fantasizing about it is not a productive use of our time. The future never materializes because it is always the present. We can never be in the future and we can never predict with 100 percent accuracy how it will unfold. Likewise, the past is history and no longer exists. It is only a memory and so clinging onto the past is equally unfruitful.

Using breath awareness as a meditative anchor is a means of "tying" the mind to the present moment. If we have not trained ourselves in mindfulness practice, then attempting to remain fully aware of the present moment without the use of a concentration anchor is probably going to be difficult. However, by gently resting our awareness on our breathing, we give the mind a reference point. The breath becomes a place the mind can return to each time it wanders off or gets lost in thoughts. You might think that becoming aware of the breath is an easy and obvious thing to do. However, be completely honest and ask yourself: how many times during the day are you truly aware of the fact that you are breathing? How often do you stop and think "I am alive and I am breathing in and out"? Because breathing happens automatically, most people tend to take it for granted.

Following the breath is a practical way to develop mindful awareness and to anchor ourselves in the present moment. In fact, breathing in and out is something that we are (hopefully) always doing, and so simply bringing our attention to the breath should not inconvenience us or require a large time commitment. However, over and above convenience, there are a number of important reasons for using the breath as a meditative anchor. Most importantly, research demonstrates that breath awareness helps to slow down the heart rate and to calm and relax the body. The body and mind are very closely related and so if we want to slow down and quieten the mind such that it can be observed and investigated, then it helps if we calm and relax the body.

There are other reasons for using the breath to stabilize the mind, and these mostly relate to some of the subtler aspects of meditation. For example, the breath is what connects the body to the world around us. Each time we breathe in, we breathe in a part of our world, and each time we breathe out, a part of us enters and joins the world around us. In fact, with each breath we take, we breathe in the wind, and since there is water vapor in the wind, we also breathe in the oceans, lakes, and rivers. Likewise, when we breathe out, parts of our breath are carried by the wind and are gradually absorbed by the world and its inhabitants. Therefore, if we decided to practice mindfulness by just sitting down quietly in a chair and simply following our breathing, with each breath in and out we would be perfectly entitled to gently self-guide our meditation by using phrases such as: "breathing in, I follow my breath in," "breathing out, I follow my breath out"; "breathing in, I breathe in the world," "breathing out, I breathe out the world"; "breathing in, I feel nourished by the earth"; "breathing out, I feel rooted in the earth."

Awareness of breathing helps to synchronize the internal winds of the body and mind with the winds of the external world. We will discuss the principle and science of interconnectedness later in this book, but a key point to remember is that using the breath to stabilize and synchronize the mind does not mean that we have to force or modify our breathing. In other words, the breath should be allowed to follow its natural course and to calm and deepen of its own accord. Forced breathing runs contrary to the general principle of meditation, which is that tranquility and wisdom are naturally present in the mind and will arise of their own accord when the correct conditions come about. One of these "correct conditions" is simply observing and nourishing the body and mind by practicing mindful awareness.

A metaphor that might help explain this notion is that of a garden fish pond. Every time the garden pond is stirred or interfered with, the water becomes muddy and disturbed. However, if a person sits quietly next to the pond and simply observes it, the water becomes perfectly still and clear again. Thus, we don't have to interfere with the mind for it to become calm and clear. All we have to do is sit in quiet and observe it.

We would like to share with you something that happened when we were guiding a meditation retreat a few years ago in the Snowdonia Mountains of North Wales. Having explained to the retreat participants how to breathe correctly and the importance of not forcing the breath, we began to guide a meditation session. One of the people seated in the meditation hall was a middle-aged lady who was extremely stressed and who desperately needed to unwind and relax. Part way through the meditation, it became apparent that one of the male participants in the group was a "breather." Breathers are those people who breathe really deeply and loudly during meditation so that everybody else can hear them, and so that everybody knows they are "serious" about their practice. About half way through the meditation session, it all became too much for the lady who broke her silence and in a frustrated voice suddenly shouted out *stop breathing.* Obviously, the lady's response was a bit excessive and everybody laughed about it later. However, it raises the point that when we are with other people, we should always consider whether our practice is cultivating—or disrupting—the harmony of the environment around us, and this includes the way we breathe.

GENEROUS BREATHING

A further important consideration relates to the type and amount of attention that we allocate toward observing our breathing. For example, there are certain types of meditation practice where the practitioner is required to focus solely on the breath or on another given object. In general, such forms of meditation involve narrowing one's attention and blocking out or ignoring other psychological or sensory experiences. However, a potential drawback of meditating in this manner is that it has limited application in real-world settings, and encourages reliance on a peaceful external environment in order to cultivate a peaceful internal environment.

If we are going to walk the path of the Mindful Warrior and face everything life throws at us with confidence and equanimity, then we need a meditative technique that is unconditionally accepting, and that is not reliant on the external environment in which we find ourselves. Therefore, when we rest our attention on the natural flow of the in-breath and out-breath, we should do so by using a very broad and generous (rather than a narrow) form of attention. In other words, mindful breathing requires us to be aware of each and every part of each and every breath, but in a way that enables us to be completely open to, and aware of, everything else that we encounter. This is why we refer to the breath as an anchor. Its purpose is to provide stability so that we can remain rooted enough to embrace and experience the present moment in all of its beauty and splendor.

It may sound as though two different forms of attention are used during mindfulness practice—a finer type of attention that focuses on the breathing, and a more expansive type of attention that encompasses and remains aware of everything else that we experience. Conceptually speaking, this may be true. However, in reality, it is not particularly helpful to bog ourselves down in trying to analyze all of the different attentional or cognitive skills utilized during mindfulness practice. Where we really need to concentrate our efforts at this stage is on starting to integrate mindfulness into all aspects of our lives and on developing an understanding of mindfulness that is based on experience and practice, and not on theory or intellectualizing.

Working on the assumption that the average respiratory rate of a healthy adult is approximately fifteen breaths per minute, this means that we breathe in and out 21,600 times each day. Every single breath in and out provides us with an opportunity to culti- vate mindful awareness and to nourish our inner being. In fact, each in-breath and out-breath could be thought of as an entirely new phase of our lives. We breathe in and are fully aware of all parts of the in-breath, from the point where it enters the body at the tips of the nostrils to the point where it gives way to the out- breath. We are intricately aware of the beginning part of the in- breath, the middle-part of the in-breath, and the final part of the in-breath. We are aware of its texture, its weight, its flavor, and its temperature. We feel the in-breath as it enters the lungs and causes them to expand. With each breath in, we feel the surge of energy that flows through our veins and nourishes every cell of the body.

Next comes the out-breath. We experience each part of the out-breath as it flows out of the body and dissolves into the air around us. However, before we breathe out, there is a brief period where the breath finds itself in no man's land. This is the period of transition between the in-breath and out-breath (and between the out-breath and in-breath) where there exists empty space that we can recognize and relax into. The more we practice mindful breathing, the more we are able to recognize this empty space and use it as a means of cultivating wisdom. We will discuss this idea in more detail later in this book but at this stage the main point to understand is that depending on our level of awareness, it is pos- sible to experience life on a breath-by-breath basis. Indeed, the more we practice breath awareness, the more we become attuned to all that happens in a single breath cycle. It is almost as though time begins to expand and the present moment starts to last long- er. Each breath in and out becomes a significant and enjoyable part of our life. This is a generous way to live and breathe, and it allows us to be continuously nourished by spiritual and meditative awareness.

THE BREATH OF THE MINDFUL WARRIOR

By remaining aware of our breathing, we equip ourselves to venture into the present moment without fear of it causing us to lose our ground or be drawn back into mindlessness and confusion. We gently rest and maintain our awareness on our breathing as we go about each of our daily tasks. If we are walking outside or in the home, we do so while calmly attending to our breathing. The same applies to working at the computer, playing with the kids, taking a shower, making love, or talking with a friend on a mobile phone— all of these activities should be conducted while trying to remain aware of each and every breath.

At first, the practice of observing the breath requires deliberate effort and it is easy to lose awareness. Don't worry or chastise yourself if you do. Upon losing awareness all we have to do is recognize that our attention has gone astray and then gently return our awareness back to the cycle of breathing. In fact, each time we notice that we have lost concentration and drifted into mindlessness, we should quietly congratulate ourselves for having recognized that the mind has wandered off again. Becoming aware of the mind's tendency to be distracted is one of the first signs that we are making progress and that our practice is moving in the right direction.

Although the practice of mindful breathing requires deliberate effort and can be quite a change from the way we normally go through the day, with sustained practice, remaining aware of the breath becomes a natural thing to do. In time, the practice starts to happen almost automatically. After we have tasted the benefits of breath awareness, we begin to see just how exposed we were to stress, confusion, and exhaustion before we adopted the practice of mindful living. When we are attending to our breathing correctly, the whole body becomes light and energized—as though we are carried by a calming wind that gently supports and stays with us wherever we go. This is consistent with scientific investigations where it has been shown that conscious breathing facilitates relaxation and leads to a slowing-down of the heart rate, respiratory rate, perspiration rate, and other bodily functions controlled by the involuntary nervous system.

Paying attention to our breathing enables us to relax into the present moment. Whatever we experience, we observe it, taste it, and enjoy it. But we also let go of it. We breathe in noticing and experiencing our external environment, and we breathe out noticing and experiencing our internal, psychological environment. Sounds come and go, sights come and go, smells come and go, sensations come and go, and thoughts and feelings come and go. Whatever happens, we remain with our breathing and let the present moment unfold around us. We observe the present moment and we also participate in it. So long as we are consciously breathing, the present moment becomes our home and we are never lost.

By anchoring ourselves in the here and now with our breathing, we construct the meditative foundations necessary for progressing along the path of the Mindful Warrior. The Mindful Warrior is able to accept and deal with whatever the present moment throws at them. This is because their breath has become their place of permanent residence. They are always aware of their breathing and therefore, they are always at home. Nothing can shake them or cause them to panic. The Mindful Warrior is unconditionally courageous and confident in everything they do. They breathe in and say to themselves, "breathing in, I am fully aware of my breathing," and they breathe out and say to themselves "breathing out, I am alive, perfectly free, and without fear." The Mindful Warrior understands that they are deeply connected with the earth around them. They understand that as they breathe in, the universe breathes in and that as they breathe out, the universe breathes out.

A GUIDED MEDITATION ON MINDFUL BREATHING

To conclude this chapter on breath awareness, we have prepared the following guided meditation on mindful breathing. You can spend as little or as much time as you wish practicing this meditation. However, whether you choose to practice for five minutes or half an hour, the most important thing is to try to practice regularly. We suggest that you try to practice this meditation two or three times each day—once in the morning when you first wake up, again in the middle of the day, and once more in the evening. Try to find somewhere quiet when you practice the meditation and please do your best to carry your practice with you when you have finished meditating.

1. Breathing in, I am fully aware that I breathe in; breathing out, I am fully aware that I breathe out.
2. Breathing in, I am aware whether my breath is deep or shallow, short or long; breathing out, I allow my breath to follow its natural course.
3. Breathing in, I enjoy breathing in; breathing out, I enjoy breathing out and I smile gently to myself.
4. Breathing in, I am fully aware of each individual moment of my breath; breathing out, I taste and experience the texture of breath.
5. Breathing in, I am aware of whether my breath is hot or cold; breathing out, I am aware of my lungs as they rise and fall.
6. Breathing in, I inhale the wind and the oceans; breathing out, I feel rooted in the earth.
7. Breathing in, as I breathe in, the universe breathes in; breathing out, as I breathe out, the universe breathes out.
8. Breathing in, I am aware of the space and time that exists between my in-breath and out-breath, and between my out-breath and in-breath; breathing out, I relax into this space and time.

9. Breathing in, there is nowhere else I need to be; breathing out, I am already home.

10. Breathing in, I enjoy being alive; breathing out, I enjoy simply being.

2

MINDLESSNESS AND THE INVERTED HALLUCINATION

In terms of its literal meaning, the word *mindfulness* could be interpreted as the practice of having a "full-up" mind. However, when practicing mindfulness, we shouldn't be aiming to fill ourselves with mental activity, concepts, and clever ideas. Too many people have their minds full, and a full mind often leads to stress and tiredness. If our minds are too full, then there is no room for wholesome thoughts to grow and flourish. In a full mind there is no room for simply being, and there is no empty space to nurture and refresh us.

On occasions when we find ourselves in front of a new intake of university students, we often ask them what they understand by the term *mindfulness*. One of the most common responses is the idea that you must be hyper-aware of the present moment. Mindfulness is a translation of the Pāli word *sati* (Sanskrit: *smrti*) which can be roughly translated as "to remember" (i.e., to remember to be aware of the present moment). However, remembering to be aware of the present moment is quite different from becoming hyper-aware or obsessed with it. Practicing mindfulness should be a natural and relaxing process, and there is no need for us to actively look for things to be aware of. As and when something arises within our field of awareness, all we need to do is to gently observe it. Instead of being "full of mind," what we should be attempting to achieve during *sati* practice is to be fully "with the mind." We do this by allowing whatever object happens to be in front of us to naturally enter our awareness. It could be an external object such as a tree or a sound, or it could be an internal object such as a thought, feeling, or emotion. Once it has entered our awareness, we sit with the object allowing it to live for a moment and, like all things, we allow it to die—to pass away.

It is not just some university students that have developed the wrong ideas about mindfulness. Indeed, for a number of years now, psychologists and academics have struggled to come to a clear understanding of mindfulness, and to agree on exactly what constitutes correct mindfulness practice. It seems that nearly every academic paper that we read about mindfulness includes a statement to the effect that *"there is currently a lack of consensus among Western psychologists in terms of how to define mindfulness."* Our personal view is that too much emphasis is placed by Western psychologists on attempting to devise and disseminate an absolute or all-encompassing definition of mindfulness.

As individuals walking the path of the Mindful Warrior, we don't need to concern ourselves too much with what constitutes a precise definition of mindfulness. We can leave those types of debates to scholars. When the Buddha taught and practiced mindfulness some twenty-five hundred years ago, he wasn't concerned with intellectualizing about mindfulness. He was only interested in practicing it. If people commit themselves to practicing mindfulness, then they will have firsthand experience of what it is (and then it won't matter how other people choose to define it).

FASHIONABLE MINDFULNESS

More and more people are becoming interested in the practice of mindfulness and some are beginning to make a living from teaching mindfulness. If people are truly living in mindful awareness then it will certainly be beneficial for themselves and for society.

However, trying too hard to spread the teachings of mindfulness may actually do more harm than good. In our opinion, if a teacher truly has a correct and authentic understanding of mindfulness, it is much better that they establish just ten followers, or even one, fully on the path of the Mindful Warrior, than have ten thousand followers whose interest remains superficial.

A few years ago, we were giving some talks about meditation and Buddhism in Southern India. It just so happened that at one of the conference venues, a mindfulness and yoga retreat was also taking place with international participants. It was easy to identify which people were involved in the retreat because the retreat participants would walk around the grounds with an air of super-iority. Their hands were invariably cupped together and held in front of them. Their head was often slightly bent to the side and most of them had a "holier than thou" smile fixed across their faces. However, it appeared that when they thought they were out of public view, they stopped behaving like this.

Mindfulness practice should enable us to become more famil-iar with the chaotic and unruly nature of the mind. The idea is that we begin to appreciate just how much ego is involved in each and every one of our thoughts and perceptions. It's when we begin to become aware of the extent to which ego has overwhelmed the mind that we can take steps to loosen the hold we have allowed the ego to have over us. The practice that the retreat participants were making was just for show. They were trying to be fashionable and keep-up with the latest spiritual trend. Indeed, for these peo-ple, rather than providing a means of spiritual development, their apparent practice of "mindfulness" was actually acting as an obsta-cle to spiritual growth. Their practice was reinforcing their ego rather than dismantling it.

It is not just lay people attending meditation retreats that dis-play this kind of behavior. Some Buddhist monks and meditation teachers fall into the same trap. It is very easy to act mindful and to hide behind robes, titles, or publication records. However, it only takes an individual embodying the Mindful Warrior princi-ples, and who is firm and resolute in their practice, to look deep

into the eyes of such individuals and understand the truth. Therefore, we should always try to be natural in our practice of mindfulness and spiritual development. We should be honest with ourselves and try not to vary our practice depending on who might be
looking.

MINDLESSNESS

We can think of mindlessness as the opposite of mindfulness.
Mindlessness refers to a lack of present-moment awareness,
whereby a person is out of touch with what they are thinking and
doing in the here and now. Consequently, a person who is mindless might be said to be engaging in the "non-perceiving of that
which is." There appears to be a strong resemblance between the
state of mindlessness and the phenomenon of hallucination. Rather than "not perceiving that which is" (i.e., mindlessness), hallucination is generally considered to be "the perceiving of that which
is not." Given that both states involve a mistaken perception of the
here and now, we have argued in some of our academic papers
that mindlessness is actually a form of inverted hallucination.

According to some Buddhist teachings, mindlessness is considered to be the default disposition of the overwhelming majority of
people. Therefore, many individuals deemed to be mentally
healthy by Western conventions (e.g., as defined by the World
Health Organization) might actually be considered 'delusional'
and suffering from a persistent form of inverted hallucination according to Buddhist theory.

The blackbird in the garden has spent many lifetimes preparing
just so we can hear its song in that exact moment of time and
space. Likewise, we have spent many lifetimes preparing so that
we can be present at that exact moment to hear what the blackbird
has to say. The same is true for all our encounters with all phenomena. However, if we allow the mundane mind—with its emotions, thoughts, feelings, and opinions—to invade that moment, it
will pass completely unacknowledged and we will remain in our

inverted hallucinatory state. The blackbird's song will be missed and life will take a completely different course, captained by the unruly mind.

The past is only a memory, the future a fantasy. All we have is this present moment, and if we are not aware of what is now, we may as well not be here. We risk becoming walking corpses that allow life to pass by completely unnoticed. The path of the Mindful Warrior is the opposite of the path of the walking corpse. The Mindful Warrior strives to be awake, aware, and fully alive during each beautiful moment of precious life.

I DON'T THINK; THEREFORE, I AM NOT

The Latin words *cogito ergo sum* (I think; therefore, I am) are attributed to the seventeenth-century French philosopher René Descartes. However, according to Descartes's logic, the following statement is also true: "*I don't think; therefore, I am not.*" Clearly, this statement is untenable, because if a person happens not to be engaged in thought, this does not, by default, mean that they don't exist (or that they are not aware that they exist). Thus, there are some flaws in Descartes's system of attributing our existence (or awareness of our existence) to the presence or absence of thought.

Indeed, whether we are thinking a lot, a little, or not at all, has very little to do with the extent to which we can say we exist and are alive. Rather than the presence or absence of thought, what is important from the Mindful Warrior's point of view is the degree to which we are aware of our thoughts. If we have thoughts but are not aware of them, then although by Descartes's criteria this still means we exist, we can't really say that we are fully aware of our existence.

In the traditional Buddhist teachings concerning mindfulness, Buddhist suttas such as the *ānāpānasati sutta*, *satipatthāna sutta*, and *kāyagatāsati sutta* refer to four different points of reference that we can use as focus points for mindfulness practice. These four points of reference are the body (including and especially the breath), feelings, thoughts, and phenomena more generally. We will discuss the practice of mindfulness in relation to these four reference points later but the main point to bear in mind is that we use mindfulness in order to become fully aware of all aspects of our existence.

Our existence is made up of that which we experience with the body and that which we experience with the mind. We interact with ourselves and the world around us through the body and mind, and so by gradually becoming aware of the four focal points mentioned above, we can ensure that important aspects of our lives are not overlooked. By cradling our bodies and minds in mindful awareness, we allow ourselves to observe and relish each moment of our existence as well as to fully participate in life. When we become a "participating observer," life starts to take on a new meaning and perspective. Being a participating observer allows us to move beyond Descartes's assertion, "I think; therefore, I am," and instead experience the truth contained in the statement, "I am fully aware of each moment of my life; therefore, I am fully alive."

THE MONKEY MIND

Within some meditation and Buddhist practice communities, the term *monkey mind* is used to describe people that have very unsettled minds. If you have a monkey mind, it basically means that, like a naughty monkey, your mind constantly jumps from one thing to another and only very rarely does it actually sit still. People with monkey minds might be engaged in some kind of task or conversation, but they quickly succumb to boredom and their mind wanders off again.

In general, people with a more severe form of monkey-mindedness are easy to identify because in addition to being mentally restless, they are invariably also physically restless. Of course, there can be many reasons, including medical ones, which may influence the degree of physical unrest that a person exhibits.

However, generally speaking, if a person finds it difficult to sit still and always has to be doing something, then this is a sign that they may have a monkey mind. Another good indicator of monkey-mindedness is when an individual is following a certain line of dialogue or conversation and they suddenly go off on tangents and introduce unrelated topics. In fact, we have met people that can thread together an endless string of completely unrelated topics and hold what they deem to be a conversation for hours, without requiring much input from anyone else. Perhaps the monkey in the mind of people like this is as big as a gorilla or perhaps it is just particularly naughty and restless—who knows?

The monkey-mind condition normally becomes apparent when people begin to practice mindfulness. People that are new to mindfulness often experience difficulty in resting their concentration on the present moment or on the natural flow of their in-breath and out-breath. This is nothing to worry about and the important thing to do when noticing we have a monkey mind is not to fight or suppress it. If we understand that, on the one hand, taming the monkey mind requires lots of effort and is arguably the most important thing we will ever do in our lives, but, on the other hand, personal and spiritual growth take time and cannot be forced, then we create the optimum frame of mind for enjoying the process of transforming unwholesome mental habits and for progressing along the path of awareness.

In order to tame the monkey mind, we need to become aware of its undisciplined nature but in a manner that keeps things light, spacious, and airy. The simple act of observing and becoming aware of our thoughts and mental processes helps to objectify them and to loosen their hold over us. However, as discussed earlier in this chapter, if we try to scrutinize our thoughts and feelings too intensely, then despite our efforts to do the opposite, we end up giving them too much power and importance. Therefore, we have to strike a balance, and the golden rule is *observe but do not cling*.

Thus, when we practice awareness of our thoughts and mental processes, we should do so with an open and generous mind. This means that we accept the mind as it is and that we don't try to manipulate it. If the mind is particularly wild and out of control, that's absolutely fine—all we do in this situation is take the unruly mind itself as the object of our awareness. In effect, what we are doing is setting the mind free within the field of our awareness. Because we are not holding onto the mind or offering it resistance by trying to keep it under control, it has no alternative but to begin to settle.

The monkey mind will remain a monkey mind for as long as we choose not to tame it. We might decide that we don't have a monkey mind or that we do have one, but that it doesn't need to be tamed. However, if we are being truthful with ourselves and if we examine the mind closely, we are likely to see that it is only very rarely (if ever) that we experience true peace of mind. Indeed, irrespective of whether we are aware of the wild nature of our mind, having a mind that is always racing around—constantly jumping to and fro between the past and the future—eventually causes us to become physically, mentally, and spiritually exhausted.

In fact, it is our personal view that mental health problems such as anxiety, stress, and depression often arise because people have unruly minds and don't know how to properly tend to their thoughts and feelings. However, it is also our view that by practicing full awareness of our thoughts and mind movements, we can begin to take care of our monkey mind until it gradually learns to sit in stillness and quiet.

TAMING THE MONKEY MIND

There are a number of contemplative exercises that can be undertaken in order to help train the monkey mind. However, before engaging in such exercises, there is an important choice that needs to be made.

In general, people subscribe to one of three different psychological strategies; they either: (i) allow their mind (with all of its emotions and mental chatter) to live their life for them, (ii) allow other people's minds (likewise full of emotions and mental chatter) to live their life for them, or (iii) choose to live their life without the interference of either their own or another persons' unruly mind. If we are serious about walking the path of the Mindful Warrior, then we have to choose, embrace, and commit to the latter strategy. By making this choice, we cultivate the right context for mindfulness practice and are thus able to see the bigger picture in terms of how specific meditative exercises fit into the wider spiritual journey that we are making.

The exercise that we would like to conclude this chapter with involves us making a "self-intervention" at the point we recognize that the monkey is running wild through the mind. In general, as people encounter different situations, thoughts and feelings automatically arise without necessarily having been summoned. For example, when standing in front of a person that is angry and shouting, most people automatically fill up with fear and start to shout back. They allow the monkey mind to take over and act out their life for them.

In situations when the monkey in our mind is misbehaving, we need to recognize that we are in danger and therefore respond by *"sending out an SOS."* The process of sending out an SOS involves repeating the following phrases to ourselves:

1. *S top*
2. *O bserve the breath*
3. *S tep back and watch the mind*

Sending out an SOS helps to interrupt our normal pattern of responding, and it creates the time and mental space necessary to evaluate what is happening in front of us. More specifically, by sending out an SOS, we create a mental sitting room where we can sit, breathe, and observe what is unfolding inside and outside of the mind. In this mental sitting room, there is only you and your breath. The mental sitting room is a safe place to be. It is a place where you can relax. The thought processes, emotions, and feelings remain outside the sitting room. If they wish to come in, they have to knock on the door.

If we don't create a sitting room in the mind, then each time we become agitated, we effectively feed the monkey mind. In fact, not only do we feed the monkey mind during the original situation that causes us to become angry, but because we tend to ruminate and cling onto things, we continue to do so for days and sometimes years after the event. Therefore, while sitting in our mental sitting room and observing the world around us, if a feeling or thought should happen to knock at the door, we check ourselves, make sure that we are relaxed, and then walk to the door without rushing. We remember that we are the host and that whoever is at the door is a guest.

Imagine that anger is knocking at the door. We gently open the door to anger and thank it for calling round. When we feel ready, we invite anger in and ask it to take a seat. We sit down directly opposite anger and we breathe, relax, and remain in silence for just a moment. Anger might be uncomfortable with the silence and it might become more agitated. However, we remain centered—and without feeling the need to say anything, we look anger straight in the eyes. When we are feeling comfortable with our guest, we can calmly ask some questions. We can ask: "Who are you exactly?" "Where do you come from?" "Why are you here?" With compassion and loving kindness, we invite our guest to talk to us. By making anger feel at home, it is easier for us to understand it. With time (and this may take multiple attempts), we begin to discover that anger, and indeed all our temporary guests, are without substance. Anger was created by us, and is still here only because we have been feeding it.

Anger will continue to return and knock at the door. However, each time we question and investigate, it becomes smaller and weaker. In fact, there may come a day when anger doesn't show up at all. The process of inviting guests into the mental sitting room requires balance and concentration. Therefore, if we find that our concentration on this guest has begun to wander, it is time to bring the conversation to a close. A wandering mind will only result in confusion. On such occasions, we stand up, thank our guest for visiting, and invite them to leave. We inform the guest that they are welcome to return at another time. We gently close the door behind anger and return to the sitting room, where there is only us and our breath.

We observe the breath in and the breath out. There is no thought of breath and no feeling of breath. There is simply breath. We experience and observe ourselves breathing in, and we experience and observe ourselves breathing out.

3

THE MINDFUL WARRIOR'S CODE

In both Eastern and Western cultures, it is drummed into people at an early age that if they are willing to push themselves and aim high, then they have a good chance of enjoying a successful life. To a large extent, this is a valid philosophy. There are almost eight billion people currently living on this earth and everybody wants a comfortable and successful life. Everybody wants a piece of the cake. However, wealth and status operate much like a pyramid and at any given time, only relatively few people can be at the top. If everybody was wealthy, the concept of wealth would no longer exist. People are only wealthy by contrast to the poor. Therefore, getting ahead of the competition invariably requires a tremendous amount of effort, determination, and focus.

It is not only with regard to wealth where the "get rich or die trying" philosophy appears to apply. Making it to the top as an athlete, business professional, artist, fashion designer, writer, actor, academic, scientist, doctor, television presenter, or journalist requires absolute focus and commitment to the task at hand. Competition is fierce, and while a small minority of people will become big names in their particular field of work, the laws of statistics mean that the majority will not.

Of course, reaching the upper echelons of the career or wealth ladder is only one means of measuring success, and some people, quite rightly, attribute success to raising a family, gaining a place at university, starting a small business, or buying a home. Others, including many in meditation and mindfulness practice circles, place less emphasis on tangible achievements. They subscribe to the view that a successful life means focusing on the journey rather than on the destination.

ATTENTION TO DETAIL

Although there are certainly advantages associated with adopting some of the abovementioned methods of relating to success (and life more generally), from the point of view of the Mindful Warrior none of these approaches quite hits the mark. Adopting the approach of focusing on the journey rather than on the destination is a nice idea, but it is also a somewhat selfish approach. The fact of the matter is that we share this world with numerous other people and living beings. Each of our thoughts, words, and actions create a ripple that continues indefinitely throughout time and space. It is all very well to just chill out and "be in the present moment" but at some point, the product of our time spent dwelling in the present moment is going to be experienced by other people.

Consequently, the Mindful Warrior is a person that fully enjoys each step of their life journey. However, by understanding that their journey will influence the lives of countless living beings, they are very much focused on the end product of their actions. If a Mindful Warrior is a painter, then while at their easel, they are fully aware of the present moment. They calmly notice each breath, each hand movement, each sound and color around them. However, they also strive—with unremitting focus—to create a masterpiece. They understand that other people will view and absorb the content of their painting, and so they inject their work with awareness, compassion, and discipline.

From this point of view, it is accurate to say that the Mindful Warrior is a person that pays attention to detail. They are wholeheartedly committed to every task they undertake. It doesn't matter if they are going to the toilet or addressing their head of state; every detail of the Mindful Warrior's life is invested with spiritual energy and meditative awareness. Their life is their practice, and they are very much engaged in this world. The Mindful Warrior doesn't particularly have time for individuals who are on some kind of enlightenment trip and who think that spiritual practice is about taking it easy or "staying in the moment."

NOT GETTING CAUGHT UP IN THE DETAIL

It is important to point out that the focus the Mindful Warrior places on the product or end result of their efforts is very different from the type of focus adopted by individuals striving to get to the top of the career or wealth pyramid. In fact, it sounds like a strange thing to say, but the Mindful Warrior's focus comes from understanding that all worldly endeavors ultimately amount to nothing. A natural law of the universe is that anything amassed or achieved will ultimately disband and fade away. The only direction that individuals at the top of the career or wealth ladder can go is down. Whatever we build up or create during our lives simply cannot endure with time, and even if it endures for a few hundred years, we certainly can't strike a deal with death in order to hang around with it.

Businesses fold, family members die, careers come to an end, buildings crumble, and policies are overwritten. The Mindful Warrior understands clearly that nothing endures and that from this perspective, all goals and undertakings are basically of the same taste. At the absolute level, all projects and endeavors—no matter how big or small—have the same level of meaning and importance. Whether creating a small flower bed in the corner of the garden or building an entire city, both of these projects have a limited lifespan. In the larger scheme of things, there are no solid grounds for arguing that one of these projects is more important than the other. The universe and the planets that it contains were born, they live and they will fade away. The beings that live upon these planets likewise come into existence, engage in all kinds of schemes and activities, and then die after a short period of time.

Due to understanding that at the ultimate level, it is impossible to create or achieve something, the Mindful Warrior remains unattached to the outcome of their work. When they create something or accomplish a goal, they understand that nothing is truly created or accomplished. The Mindful Warrior knows that phenomena change in the moment we observe them and that whatever currently is, will ultimately cease to exist. Therefore, an important part of the Mindful Warrior's code is the ability to combine the seemingly contradictory principles of paying close attention to the details of their life without getting caught up in those details.

FEARLESSNESS

Some people are of the view that in order to enter the spiritual path one has to forget about the world and everything we know. However, rather than forgetting about or turning one's back on the world, a true spiritual practitioner completely surrenders themselves to, and becomes fully immersed in, the world. In order to surrender ourselves to the world, we first have to abandon hope and fear. When we have hope, we leave ourselves exposed to suffering. We suffer when our hopes and expectations are not met. Wherever there is hope, there is also fear—the fear that our hopes will not be realized.

Many people think that in order to be happy they need hope. But this kind of happiness is conditional. It is reliant upon the presence of external factors. Relying on external factors will never lead to lasting happiness because situations and phenomena are changing all the time and there is no way that we can control them all. By always hoping to be somewhere else, be someone else, or have something else, we effectively turn our back on the present moment, and deep spiritual peace can never take root in the mind. This is not to say that we should not make efforts to improve our current situation but we should not allow the mind to intoxicate itself with hope that our efforts will bear fruit. In other words, if we wish to change or improve our current circumstances, we should do so with absolute focus to the task at hand but should remain unattached to the idea that we are somehow going to gain something or get somewhere.

It is by engaging in, yet remaining unattached to, all they experience that the Mindful Warrior creates the correct conditions for gaining their first taste of unconditional fearlessness. When they have become adept at abandoning hope and desire, absolutely nothing can shake the Mindful Warrior's confidence. Without trying, the Mindful Warrior begins to emanate strength, courage, and contentedness. They remain centered and unfazed by any situation. People can't help but notice the fearlessness that exudes from an authentic Mindful Warrior. However, because the Mindful Warrior's fearlessness stems from a place of calm, compassion, and non-attachment, people invariably feel reassured and safe in the Mindful Warrior's presence.

Of course, there will always be a small minority of people who feel threatened and unsettled in the presence of a Mindful Warrior, whose attitude is so different to theirs. The Mindful Warrior's calmness and clarity of mind holds up a mirror to their own mind, and some won't be ready to see that there is no substance to the self they have worked so hard to create. If they do feel threatened, they may become angry. But others will use it as a constructive opportunity to examine their life and make changes where appropriate.

The quality of fearlessness that arises naturally as part of walking the path of the Mindful Warrior stems from a place of wisdom, compassion., and freedom from hope. It has absolutely nothing to do with being macho or deliberately trying to be courageous. These types of fearlessness are very much reliant on the presence of a "me," a "mine," and an "I." The fearlessness that exudes from the Mindful Warrior is what is left after these are removed from the equation. For this reason, the Mindful Warrior's fearlessness is devoid of aggression and is without a personal agenda.

An important source of the Mindful Warrior's fearlessness is absolute commitment to the path that they are walking. The Mindful Warrior does not make a distinction between spiritual practice and time at work or time with the family. Whatever they are doing and wherever they find themselves, they strive to perfect each breath, moment, and activity of their lives. This unremitting commitment to their chosen path provides them with access to an immense resource of spiritual energy. It is the energy of the present moment that flows through and connects all phenomena.

By tapping into and nourishing themselves in this energy, the Mindful Warrior is able to respond with fearlessness and take whatever happens in their stride. Everything that they encounter forms part of their practice. It doesn't matter if they are seen as a national hero or if they are despised and ridiculed—the Mindful Warrior has absolute confidence in what they are doing. This is a beautiful and invigorating way to live.

JOYFULNESS

A further and related aspect of the Mindful Warrior's code is the ability to remain joyful in every situation. There is no such thing as a life without challenges, and encountering adverse conditions is part of being human. However, whether a situation is perceived as enjoyable or difficult depends upon our frame of mind. By seeing everything we encounter in life as a teacher, the Mindful Warrior is able to move beyond the notion of a situation being agreeable or unpleasant. In other words, they accept what is in front of them and relate to it purely on the level of experience. No one experience is better than another. All experiences present themselves as a teacher and are an opportunity to grow.

If the Mindful Warrior loses their job or reputation, that's absolutely fine. They breathe in and fully experience the situation. They breathe out and fully accept the situation. They embrace the change in their circumstances, and if need be, they take remedial action. However, they don't consider themselves in any way hard done to and they don't panic or become depressed. In fact, they thoroughly enjoy the situation.

It sounds like a difficult thing to do but being able to enjoy adverse situations is simply a matter of having the right attitude. Most people are conditioned to respond to difficult circumstances with fear, panic, and aggression. Having observed their parents, friends, and peers respond in this manner, they begin to acquire the same habit. Without realizing it, people "practice" responding to adversity with negative emotions, and before long, they become experts in this way of handling the various problems of their life. However, it is entirely possible to break this automatic reaction to adversity.

The first step toward doing this involves recognizing the fear and panic response as soon as it begins to arise. If we wish to change a behavioral response pattern that has become deep-seated in our minds, we first need to become aware of it. This is where being mindful of each of our thoughts and feelings comes in. By simply recognizing that we are beginning to panic or become frightened, we already start to disrupt the mind's normal pattern of being embroiled in thoughts and emotions.

We can disrupt these maladaptive response patterns by attending to our breathing, and by making an effort to be strong and present with ourselves. However, more importantly, we should simply make the choice not to respond with fear, anger, or another destructive emotion. If we make this choice with enough conviction, it is not so difficult to interrupt our habitual and conditioned response patterns and to completely change our perspective on the situation. In the face of chaos or unwanted news, we can train ourselves to step back, relax, and thoroughly enjoy the situation. By allowing clarity and equanimity to arise in the mind, we are able to understand that it is neither a good situation nor a bad situation. It is just simply what is. There is nothing to lose and there is nothing to gain.

When we successfully manage to respond in this manner on a few occasions, we can become more confident in our ability to walk the path of the Mindful Warrior, and being unconditionally joyful eventually becomes our natural way of being. While others panic around us, we remain as solid as a mountain, with our feet firmly rooted in the earth. This is one of the reasons why we have chosen to refer to the authentic mindfulness practitioner as a warrior—being unconditionally joyful requires a great deal of courage.

The above manner of handling adverse situations may sound like a difficult thing to do. However, if you stop and think about it, there is never an instance in our lives when it is helpful to respond with panic or negativity. If there is something we can do to alleviate difficult circumstances, then we should take the appropriate action in a deliberate, focused, and calm manner. However, if there is nothing to be done, then there is no point in losing sleep over it. Doing so will not only increase the intensity of our suffering but it will impair our ability to work through the situation. There is a saying that stress is like a rocking horse—you can ride it as much as you like but it won't get you anywhere.

There is perhaps one final detail that is worth clarifying regarding the practice of unconditional joy. Being unconditionally joyful does not mean walking around all day wearing a beaming smile. Earlier in this book we referred to the tendency of some mindfulness practitioners to attempt exactly this. However, rather than genuine joyfulness, this type of behavior normally indicates a lack of conviction in one's practice. That is not to say that the Mindful Warrior does not smile. The Mindful Warrior has a beautiful smile, and they use it a lot. They smile from their heart and when they do so, they offer all of their being to the recipient of their smile. However, the Mindful Warrior knows when it is appropriate to smile and when it is not. Indeed, when the situation calls for it, the Mindful Warrior can be fierce and unremitting—but this doesn't mean that there is not contentedness and joy in their heart.

A HUMBLE SERVANT

Another important aspect of the Mindful Warrior's code is humility. The Mindful Warrior is uninterested in being recognized or rewarded. This is not to say that they cannot accept recognition, but it certainly isn't something they consider when deciding on a course of action. In fact, by staying out of the limelight, it is often much easier for the Mindful Warrior to be effective at gently guiding others along the spiritual path.

The Mindful Warrior understands that, much like a spider's web that spreads out in a full circle, they are deeply connected to all other lifeforms and phenomena in the universe. They see each and every encounter with another lifeform as a very important event and they understand that their thoughts, words, and actions will have an impact on the future wellbeing of on that, as well as every other, lifeform. Consequently, the Mindful Warrior is a humble servant of each and every living being on the planet.

It does not matter whether the Mindful Warrior meets or interacts with a supermarket cashier, neighbor, work colleague, famous person, partner, criminal, dog, cat, butterfly, or even an individual wishing them harm, they are fully present for that being. By being sincere, humble, and fully aware in that being's presence, the Mindful Warrior provides that person or being with exactly what they need at that particular moment in their life in order to help them advance along the spiritual path.

Another important part of the Mindful Warrior's practice of humility is to see themselves as a student of every person and situation they encounter. Being a humble person allows the Mindful Warrior's mind to remain supple enough to learn from every situation. They see everything they do as an opportunity to learn and they see every situation as their teacher. They are able to derive profound meaning and significance even from simple acts such as breathing in and out, putting one foot in front of the other, or watching the leaves fall from the tree.

If the Mindful Warrior happens to have students of their own, they are also a student of their students. In no way does the Mindful Warrior think that they are superior to another person. They interact with their students and with everybody they meet at the level of a spiritual being. The Mindful Warrior is one spiritual being and, whether the other person knows it or not, they are another spiritual being. Neither party is more important than the other. Both parties are vital components of the universe.

However, being a student and servant to all does not mean that the Mindful Warrior allows others to use them as a doormat. Doing so would not be in anybody's best interests. Thus, the Mindful Warrior understands that in order to be an effective servant, they may have to assert their authority with certain people or in certain situations.

GRACE

A swan is elegant and graceful in its movements. It glides through the water and barely disturbs it. The Mindful Warrior is like a swan in the way they move and interact with the world. When a Mindful Warrior sits down, they know that they are sitting. They sit down deliberately and with grace of movement. They sit with their back relaxed but straight, and they hold their head centrally and confidently. The Mindful Warrior doesn't slouch when they sit down. They don't fidget with things or allow their legs or feet to bounce around. If they are unable to sit upright due to bodily pain or a physical disability, they adapt and do their best to remain composed. When a Mindful Warrior sits, they emanate presence, strength, and elegance.

The same applies to how the Mindful Warrior walks, eats, and talks. When a Mindful Warrior walks, they know that they are walking and they observe and experience the weight transfer from one foot to the other. The Mindful Warrior walks with their back straight but relaxed, and their head high. When the Mindful Warrior eats, they chew and thoroughly taste each mouthful of food. They are never in a rush to finish their meal. They eat quietly and gracefully. Likewise, when the Mindful Warrior is talking, they know that they are talking. They never open their mouth without being aware of what they are about to say. Others may try to draw the Mindful Warrior into their soap opera, but the Mindful Warrior remains aware, confident, and graceful.

By perfecting their practice, the Mindful Warrior creates an atmosphere of spiritual presence and this helps others to calm and connect with their own capacity for being awake to the present moment. This is consistent with findings from research investigating how a teacher's mindfulness practice affects the behavior of their students.[1] Findings from such studies point toward an almost "contagious" property of mindfulness and suggest that just by being in the presence of mindfulness practitioners, children and adolescents experience enhanced levels of wellbeing and start to become increasingly aware of how to behave in a manner considered to be more psychologically and socially adaptive.

SIMPLY BEING WITH NOTHING TO BE

From time to time, we engage in writing a type of spiritual song or poem called a *vajragiti*. The Sanskrit word *vajra* means "diamond" or "indestructible" and the word *giti* means "song." Some of our *vajragitis* have been spoken or written spontaneously, while others have been written at the request of a particular person or for a particular occasion.

The following *vajragiti* that we wrote follows a structure of four verses of four lines and is called "Simply Being with Nothing to Be." This *vajragiti* includes two Sanskrit words, *Apranihita* and *Dharmadhatu*, which respectively mean "desirelessness" and "the realm of unconditioned truth."

> *Nowhere to go, nothing to do*
> *No reputation to build, none to defend*
> *No possessions to amass, none to protect*
> *This is fearlessness born of Apranihita*
>
> *Simply here, simply now*

Simply birth, simply death
Simply content, simply aware
Simply abiding, simply being

No space, no time
So no here, no now
No self, no other
So no attachment, no aversion

Letting go with nothing to let go of
Practice with no path to walk
Simply being with nothing to be
This is the all-pervading wisdom of Dharmadhatu

4

CARRY YOUR MEDITATION CUSHION WITH YOU

Have you taken a moment today to ask yourself where your mind is? Is your mind light and free or are you holding on to things? Are you breathing in a beautiful way? Are you being kind and gentle with yourself? Are you here and are you now? These are examples of questions that we can ask ourselves each day to help us remember our practice and avoid falling back into mindless ways of living. In this chapter, we discuss some useful strategies for helping mindfulness become our natural way of being rather than something that we practice from time to time.

RECHARGING THE BATTERIES

As individuals on the path of the Mindful Warrior, it is helpful to intersperse the day with periods of seated meditation practice. In much the same manner that it is necessary to plug in and recharge a mobile phone, it is also necessary to dedicate some time in order to refocus and nourish the mind. The Mindful Warrior needs to be humble enough to know when it is time to recharge their batteries. These periods of time spent in "formal meditation" can be as short or as long as we wish to make them.

One of the most important considerations regarding seated meditation is that it should be a productive use of our time. Some people that call themselves meditation practitioners sit in meditation numerous times each day and for hours at a time. They do this for months or even years on end. However, based on the people we have met who adopt this practice (which includes some fully ordained Buddhist monks and nuns), few are making good use of their time.

A common mistake during meditation practice is to enter into what is perhaps best described as a form of daydream. In this mental state, the mind alters between periods of ruminative thinking and a kind of foggy daze. It might be possible to happen upon something that resembles genuine meditative calm while meditating in this manner, but the tendency is for the mind to become anaesthetized by these tranquil feelings. This prevents more profound states of meditative awareness from arising.

During one of our visits to Sri Lanka, we received a phone call from some rather distraught monastic colleagues who requested our attendance at a meditation retreat they were conducting. They were experiencing some difficulty with the retreat participants, who had decided to follow their own practice program and who were reluctant to take advice from the monks. The group in question was taking part in a two-week meditation retreat and comprised approximately fifteen individuals from various countries who had, by their own account, been meditating for many years. During our first meeting, the participants informed us that while engaged in formal meditation, they follow a rule of not making even the slightest bodily movement, and that they can sit in such a manner for hours on end.

A few hours after our arrival at the meditation center, it was time for the evening meditation session. The retreat participants had requested that we give a Dharma talk (i.e., teachings) after the evening meditation had finished. We sat quietly on some chairs at the back of the meditation hall and observed the group as they settled into meditation. The gong sounded to mark the start of the meditation session and, as good as their word, the participants sat so still they looked like statues. This went on for about thirty minutes, but because it was becoming stiflingly hot inside the meditation hall, we decided to quietly get up and open the door and windows. Shortly after that, an old stray dog wandered in and started exploring the meditation hall. The dog was quite smelly and started to sniff (and in some case lick the arms) of some of the participants who were sitting on cushions on the floor.

For about the first five minutes after the dog had strolled in, the participants tried to keep a straight face and not let the dog disturb them. However, it didn't take long before they began to scratch, twitch, cough, adjust their posture, and become visibly agitated. You could almost hear their thoughts: *That dog stinks and is probably full of fleas. I wonder if stray dogs here carry rabies. What happens if it bites me? I'll definitely have to go to hospital. Oh my God, it's really close to my face. I'm going to have to shoo away. Which idiot decided to open the door? Which idiot made up this rule of not moving? As soon as this torture is finished, I'm going to take a shower and disinfect my arms.*

In the midst of this physical and mental movement, the gong suddenly sounded to mark the end of the meditation session. As soon as the participants were outside of the meditation hall, they demanded to know who had opened the door and ruined their meditation practice by letting a "stupid old dog" come in. We informed them it was us who had opened the door and gently suggested that had they been meditating properly, the dog would not have been able to interfere with their practice. We offered our view that it is the mind and not the body that must sit in stillness during meditation. We then suggested to the participants that they were not making productive use of their time during meditation and that they should start from the beginning. We also informed them that in respect of giving a Dharma talk, the dog had provided them with a far more valuable lesson than we might have been able to impart during an hour of talking. We likewise shared our view that the dog they considered to be "old" and "stupid" might be their greatest teacher.

We left shortly after but were a little concerned that we may have been too firm. However, we received a phone call a few days later from the monk overseeing the retreat, who informed us that the participants' attitude—and the retreat atmosphere more generally—was much improved. During the phone call we also enquired as to the whereabouts and wellbeing of the dog. However, the dog was completely unknown to the people in the temple and local villages, and nobody had seen it since it walked out of the meditation hall at the point the gong sounded.

BEING PRODUCTIVE IN MEDITATION

The starting point for making meditation practice productive—particularly at the beginning stages—is adopting a good physical posture. As we touched on in chapter 3, a slouched bodily posture tends to lead to a slouched mind, and a bodily posture that is too uptight and rigid tends to lead to an agitated mind. When guiding meditation retreats, something we see time and time again is people coming into the meditation on the first day and sitting with their backs rigidly straight and with a face as cold as ice. On one occasion when this happened, we asked the retreat participants to go back to their rooms and return when they had found a little joy and were more relaxed. We also asked them to consider smiling now and again.

Thus, the correct posture for meditation is one that is stable—neither too tight nor too loose. Stability can be achieved whether sitting upright on a chair or on a meditation cushion. When you sit in meditation, remain upright and hold your posture, but don't make yourself tense. The analogy that we often use for the correct meditation posture is that of a mountain. A mountain has a definite presence, it is upright and stable yet at the same time it is without tension. A mountain does not have to strain to maintain its posture. It is relaxed, content, and deeply rooted in the earth.

After having adopted a suitable physical posture, the next thing to do is to allow the mind to move deeper into meditation in as natural a manner as possible. One gently attends to one's breathing, without forcing it in any way, and allows the mind to start to relax and open up. There shouldn't be any expectation that the meditation session will be particularly rewarding or that some profound experience will arise. Just allow the session to move along at its own pace. Some meditation sessions might seem more rewarding than others. That's fine. Try not to judge them. Just focus on being aware of what is in front of you.

As the mind continues to calm and collect itself, one can then allow meditative awareness to grow and expand. While maintaining awareness of the in-breath and out-breath, become aware of the body and everything that is happening within it. Become aware of the rising and falling of the lungs, the heartbeat, and the blood that is pulsing through the veins. Become aware of the body's weight and the point where it makes contact with the seat or meditation cushion below you. Gently allow your awareness to infuse each cell of the body, and allow the body to bathe in meditative calm. Breathe in being fully aware of the body, and breathe out allowing the body to relax.

With the body grounded and bathed in meditative calm, meditative awareness can be allowed to expand even further. The body is not an isolated entity. It is deeply connected with the earth and all other phenomena. Therefore, try to follow and stay with your breath as it leaves the body. Know that your breath permeates the air around you and that it spreads out in a thousand different directions. Likewise, know that, each moment, your body is processing and digesting your last meal. Your last meal came from, and was part of, the earth. Now it is in your body—the earth has become you. Therefore, when you expand your meditative awareness in order to encompass the body, you should feel and be aware that your body is really the entire earth. Breathe in being fully aware of the earth, and breathe out allowing the earth to relax.

After establishing yourself in awareness of breath and awareness of body, you can begin to establish yourself in awareness of your feelings, thoughts, and other mental processes. This doesn't mean that you forget about being aware of the body and the breath. They just move into the background a little bit to enable you to redirect your focus. When practicing awareness of feelings and of the movements of the mind, all one has to do is to notice them. At this point, there is no need to investigate them. Simply cradle them with meditative awareness. Breathe in, fully aware of your feelings and thoughts, and breathe out, allowing them to relax.

As we observe our breath, body, feelings, and thoughts, they begin to calm and gradually slow down. This happens naturally and it is not something that we should try to force. Exposing the body and mind to meditative awareness creates a lot of psychological space inside and around us, and we can remain in this space for as short or as long a period as we wish. As we become more experienced in meditation, it becomes easier to reestablish ourselves in this space.

Eventually, we reach a point where the feelings of calm produced during meditation become very pronounced. This is a good place to start investigating the mind as well as the true manner in which we, and the phenomena around us, actually exist. However, for now, we will limit the discussion to calming the body and mind. We will explore the practice of investigative or analytical meditation a little later in the book.

MAINTAINING MEDITATIVE AWARENESS

It is wonderful and revitalizing to experience true meditative calm. It is completely different from most people's understanding of what it means to be still and calm. However, despite the profound peace that can be accessed during sitting meditation, meditation practice doesn't stop at the end of a given session. In fact, it is when we blow out our candles and stand up from our cushion or chair that meditation practice truly begins. We should try not to create a separation between formal meditation sessions and everyday living. The goal is to retain your meditative awareness while (for example) traveling on a congested train, writing at the computer, watching television, or playing with your children. It is for this reason that some meditation teachers tell their students to carry their meditation cushions with them at all times (the advice is not meant to be taken literally!).

Some people find that "mindfulness reminders" can be a useful tool to help integrate mindfulness practice into daily living. An example of a mindfulness reminder is an hour chime or a watch beep, which can be used as a trigger to gently bring one's awareness back to the present moment and to the natural flow of the in-breath and out-breath (and to the space and time between each in-breath and out-breath). There are also mindfulness reminder apps that can be downloaded onto a computer or mobile phone and that make (for example) a singing-bowl sound at predesignated intervals.

About fifteen years ago, we lived at a Buddhist Monastery in the Snowdonia National Park of North Wales. There were several rescue dogs at the monastery, including a small ginger-haired crossbreed called Vajra. Vajra had been with us since he was a puppy, and he had become familiar with the practice of everybody taking a moment to stop and breathe whenever the clock chimed. Around the time of his second birthday, Vajra started to join in with the practice—he would pause for a short time whenever the clock chimed. When people visited the monastery, they would sometimes forget that the grandfather clock was used as a mindfulness reminder, and they would continue talking or darting around. On occasions when this happened, Vajra would often bark at them. It seemed he was telling them to come back to their breathing, and to the present moment.

Rather than audible prompts, some mindfulness practitioners prefer a reminder such as a simple acronym instead of a sensory cue. A good example is the SOS technique that we introduced at the end of chapter 2. One sends out an SOS (Stop; Observe the breath; Step back and watch the mind) at the point intrusive thoughts arise in the mind. However, although these reminders can be useful aids, it is not necessary to use them. If they work for you, that's great but if not, don't worry about it. They are not everybody's cup of tea.

There is a lot of scientific evidence that supports the approach of maintaining meditative awareness as we go about our various activities. For example, in the psychological literature there is a concept known as "dispositional mindfulness." Dispositional mindfulness refers to the natural or enduring level of mindfulness a person has rather than a temporary level that expires at the end of a meditation session. Dispositional mindfulness is therefore sometimes referred to as a person's "trait" level of mindfulness rather than their "state" level. Studies have shown that people with higher levels of dispositional mindfulness are less likely to be overcome by anxiety or stressful life situations. Similarly, in our own research based on the eight-week Meditation Awareness Training intervention, those who manage to integrate mindfulness practice into daily living tend to be the ones who show the greatest improvements in overall levels of psychological and spiritual wellbeing.

THERE IS ONLY ONE MINDFULNESS

In both Western psychological and traditional Buddhist settings, mindfulness techniques have been developed that are intended to be practiced in particular contexts or while engaging in specific activities. For example, some Buddhist traditions advocate that individuals engage in the practices of eating meditation, walking meditation, sitting meditation, and working meditation. Likewise, within psychology, there are many different mindfulness-based interventions that focus on the therapeutic use of mindfulness for people with (for example) stress (e.g., Mindfulness-Based Stress Reduction), depression (Mindfulness-Based Cognitive Therapy), eating disorders (Mindfulness-Based Eating Awareness Therapy), substance use disorders (Mindfulness-Based Relapse Prevention), and trauma-related issues (Mindfulness-Based Mental Fitness Training). Mindfulness-based interventions have also been developed that are not necessarily intended to treat mental health issues (e.g., interventions formulated in order to help people navigate giving birth and bringing up a child, or to excel as business leaders, etc.).

There is certainly some value in having different mindfulness techniques for specific purposes. However, the numerous techniques and interventions could give the impression that there are many different types of mindfulness. Yet, the Buddha only taught one type of mindfulness. Therefore, when we are working and decide to have lunch, it is not the case that our "working meditation" ends, and our "eating meditation" begins. Rather, we just carry the same practice of mindfulness with us wherever we go.

The exact same principle applies to using mindfulness to respond to feelings of stress, anger, low mood, or other negative states. Rather than alternate between different forms of mindfulness, we simply attend to our breathing and to whatever happens to be moving through our field of awareness. The danger with compartmentalizing mindfulness into different types of practice is that we will always see mindfulness as a practice—as something external that we apply in particular situations.

The tendency to regard mindfulness as an external practice is one of the main reasons why we generally discourage individuals from setting themselves a rigid routine of meditation practice. Some people tell us that they practice meditation at exactly the same time each day. They have their meditation time in the morning and they have a time for meditation in the evening. Perhaps some individuals benefit from this kind of fixed structure, but the truth is that each day is different from the last. Unexpected things happen, and we need to be dynamic and able to respond to situations as they unfold. A problem with having fixed times for meditation is that if for some reason we happen to miss a meditation session, we may feel underprepared, irritable, or disoriented. In other words, there is a risk that we become dependent on the routine, without attending to the real benefits of carrying our cushion with us through the day.

Part of our research has focused on examining the applications of mindfulness for treating individuals addicted to work, sex, or gambling.[1] Although preliminary findings show that mindful awareness is an effective treatment for behavioral addiction, during a particular phase of their treatment, there is evidence to suggest that some participants become mildly dependent on their meditation routine. In other words, it appears that they substitute their addiction to work, sex, or gambling for an addiction to meditation. It could be argued that addiction to work, sex, or gambling constitutes a negative addiction, whereas being addicted to meditation is a positive addiction. In relative terms, this is probably correct, but in the long term, becoming dependent upon meditation will hinder our spiritual progress.

We are certainly not saying that there is something wrong with having a daily routine of practicing meditation. However, we should strive to be flexible and remain unattached to that routine. A mother can't realistically tell her baby who has woken up earlier than normal to stop crying and wait until she has finished meditating. She has to be accommodating and work with what is happening in front of her. We want to get to the point where mindful awareness is a part of who we are, and something that we naturally embody and emanate. This will take time to develop, but if we start off with the right attitude, we can avoid falling into habits that will cause problems and hold us back further down the line.

THE RIGHT INTENTION

As we progress along the path of the Mindful Warrior, it is easy to fall into the habit of beating ourselves up because we believe we haven't practiced enough, or because we think we are moving too slowly. Similarly, some people may experience periods when energy levels are lagging or when the motivation to continue is less forthcoming. At times like this, it is useful to take a step back and remind ourselves what walking the path of the Mindful Warrior is all about.

We have chosen to walk this path for some very simple reasons. Probably the most important reason is because we have understood that continuing to live out our lives as a soap opera isn't going to get us anywhere. Before we embarked on the Mindful Warrior's path and while still caught up in soap opera living, we sensed or understood, perhaps intuitively, that there was a different way to live our lives. We started to realize that it is possible to progress to a state where suffering no longer exists.

Another reason that might have inspired us to enter the path of the Mindful Warrior was seeing the suffering in others, and wanting to do something about it. A lot of people, including many still caught up in soap opera living, are inspired to dedicate some time toward helping reduce suffering in the world. In many respects, this is a laudable thing to do. However, we should be conscious of our motivations. Are we working for others' benefit, or in order to feel better about ourselves?

When we engage in helping others without having transcended our ego, the amount of good that we can do is limited. People that are still immersed in suffering (and thus yet to transcend the self) are unlikely to be able to make wise choices about what is best for another person's long-term wellbeing. With the ego still making part of the equation, it is difficult to be completely unconditional when we do something for another person. There is invariably some kind of personal agenda that influences who we help and how much we help them. The interference of the ego tends to act as a barrier, preventing a true human-to-human or heart-to-heart interaction from taking place.

Therefore, the Mindful Warrior understands that if they truly wish to help others, they first need to help themselves. Help and kindness should be offered to others at all stages of the Mindful Warrior's journey—including right from the very beginning. However, by understanding the importance of their own path and of helping people experience unconditional rather than temporary happiness, the Mindful Warrior avoids being overwhelmed and consumed by other people's suffering.

When we approach the practices of meditation and mindfulness with the underlying intention of helping both ourselves and others permanently overcome suffering, our reasons for walking the path of the Mindful Warrior remain clear and uncomplicated. If we become confused about what we are doing and why we are doing it, we can just step back, take some breaths in awareness, and remind ourselves of our original intentions. When we take the time to ground ourselves in this manner, life and spiritual practice become simple and straightforward again. We remember that we are born, we live for a short while, and then we die. In recollecting this simple truth, we also remember that we have courageously chosen to dedicate our remaining time on this earth toward helping ourselves and others grow in spiritual wisdom.

The more we familiarize ourselves with this underlying intention to progress (and help others to progress) spiritually, the more it starts to permeate our being. Eventually, there comes a point when this intention becomes so clear that it is no longer something we need to think about. It becomes a part of who we are, and without consciously thinking about it, each of our thoughts, words, and actions becomes imbued with spiritual awareness, gentleness, and loving-kindness. Everything we do becomes meaningful because it all stems from a right intention at the core of our being. At this point on the path of the Mindful Warrior, we have learned to "carry our meditation cushion" with us at all times. To a certain degree, spiritual awareness has become self-sustaining. When this happens, there is no such thing as regret. All choices and actions are right. We still need to develop experience in the art of channeling spiritual awareness so that it really begins to benefit beings, but to all intents and purposes, all our actions are fundamentally wholesome.

The freedom, deep sense of contentment, and spiritual energy that arises from having cultivated a right intention is what we were trying to express in the following poem that we wrote called "The Offspring of Spring":[2]

Nurtured by nature
In the wild I dwell
A contented heart
But no one to tell

The heir of the air
I float on the clouds
Such freedom such bliss
No hustle no crowds

The son of the sun
Ablaze with pure light
Neverending joy
That brightens the night

The offspring of spring
Alive and aware
Transmitting the truth
Without fear or care

5

A SPIRITUAL AFFAIR

In recent decades, some definitions of mindfulness have been proposed that, in our opinion, fail to acknowledge some key attributes of mindfulness. Jon Kabat-Zinn is a well-known mindfulness teacher who during a discussion with us, was reluctant to refer to mindfulness as a spiritual faculty, instead preferring to define it as a form of "mind-body medicine." Likewise, in the contemporary psychological literature, there appears the term "mindfulness meditation." However, "mindfulness meditation" doesn't appear in the Buddhist canonical literature because mindfulness is a practice that regulates concentration during meditation (i.e., mindfulness is not meditation in and of itself).

We recently formulated the following alternative definition of mindfulness: *Mindfulness is the process of maintaining a full, direct, and active awareness of experienced phenomena that is (i) spiritual in aspect and (ii) maintained from one moment to the next.*[1] Although this delineation of mindfulness is gradually being used and cited in the academic literature, it was never intended to serve as an absolute definition. We introduced it principally for the purpose of reminding people of the traditional Buddhist (and therefore spiritual) roots of mindfulness.

In the Buddhist *suttas*, "right mindfulness" appears as the seventh aspect of the fundamental teaching known as the Noble

Eightfold Path. Immediately after "right mindfulness" comes "right concentration," which is sometimes translated as "right meditation." If the Buddha intended mindfulness to be identical to meditation, then logic dictates that he would not have introduced mindfulness and meditation as two separate aspects of the Noble Eightfold Path. Rather, he would have simply taught the Noble Sevenfold Path in which mindfulness and meditation were merged into a single path element. Therefore, as far as the Buddhist teachings are concerned, right mindfulness is not right meditation, and right meditation is not right mindfulness.

Although Buddhism asserts that mindfulness and meditation are distinct from each other, these practices are intricately interconnected. For example, in order to maintain meditative concentration on a particular object of mind (e.g., the breath, body, or present moment more generally), mindfulness needs to be present in order to recognize when the mind begins to wander, and to bring the mind back to its object of meditation. Likewise, in the absence of meditative concentration, mindfulness does not exist, because the whole point of mindfulness is to ensure that meditative concentration remains intact.

In this chapter, we explore each of the key terms introduced in our above description of mindfulness. However, we would like to clarify that our purpose for so doing is to foster understanding of mindfulness in order to help individuals advance along the path of the Mindful Warrior. As mentioned above, from the Buddhist perspective and technically speaking, mindfulness is effectively the process of ensuring that meditative concentration remains intact. Thus, our above depiction of mindfulness is somewhat holistic and is intended to demonstrate that mindfulness is a practice that takes place in the context of a wider process of meditative and spiritual development. Therefore, if you happen to like this description of mindfulness, then that's great, but try not to cling to it. Equally, if you think it is an unsatisfactory definition, that's okay. Just treat it (and the discussion that follows) as food for thought, and then let it go.

FULL AWARENESS

Full awareness refers to the encompassing and passive aspects of mindfulness. By *encompassing* we mean that when practicing mindfulness, mindful attention should be directed to everything that enters the field of awareness. A 'mindfulness anchor' such as observing the breath can be used to steady and collect the mind. However, rather than make the breath the exclusive focus of awareness, the idea is to use the breath to anchor the mind so that we can embrace the full depth and beauty of the present moment. As exemplified by the following extract from the *Ānāpānasati Sutta*,[2] full awareness means that whatever we are doing, we should strive to be present with ourselves:

> Again, a Mindful Warrior is one who acts in full awareness when going forward and returning; who acts in full awareness when looking ahead and looking away; who acts in full awareness when flexing and extending his limbs; . . . who acts in full awareness when eating, drinking, consuming food and tasting; who acts in full awareness when defecating and urinating; who acts in full awareness when walking, standing, sitting, falling asleep, waking up, talking and keeping silent.

In essence, being fully aware means that we are awake and paying attention during all aspects of our lives. Wherever we are and whatever we are doing, we should strive to be fully aware of our inner and external environment. In this manner, our whole life becomes one big practice of meditative awareness. Things become simple and uncomplicated again. We can see the big picture but we can also see how each individual phenomenon and movements of mind contributes to this picture. Due to being aware of what is happening both inside and outside of ourselves, we always have our bearings and we always know what we should be doing.

Counterintuitively, full awareness actually helps us to empty the mind. We can empty the mind because there is no longer any ambiguity in terms of who we should be, what we should do, what we should say, or where we should go. We practice full awareness of life as it is in the here and now and we experience happiness and contentment. We are able to relax because we see and understand that life in the here and now is always complete. It contains everything that we could ever require; nothing is lacking.

Full awareness can be described as being passive because when practicing mindfulness, there is no need to look for things to be aware of. We simply observe physiological, psychological, and spiritual experiences as they enter our awareness. This aspect of mindfulness practice is gentle and uncontrived, and it is accepting of every experience that we encounter. If we are sitting in the garden and a bird lands on the branch of a nearby tree and sings for us, we can smile at the bird and listen to every note of its song. However, we don't need to go looking for the bird or strain ourselves in order to see or hear everything that is happening around us. If we try to practice mindfulness by actively looking and searching for things, we will not only introduce tension into our being, but also into the environment and lifeforms around us. The bird will sense that we are trying to force or modify the present moment, and it may become frightened and fly away.

As you might have already guessed, the *Ānāpānasati Sutta* that we referred to above doesn't actually use the term *Mindful Warrior*. Instead, it uses the word *Bhikkhu* which is a Pāli word meaning "Buddhist monk." However, we should read the Buddhist teachings in such a manner that allows us to relate to them and that makes them easy to digest. Therefore, if it makes you feel more comfortable, it is okay to exchange the word *Bhikkhu* for the word *Mindful Warrior* when you read the Buddhist suttas. Alternatively, if you like, you can change the word *Bhikkhu* for another word that better fits you. For example, you could exchange the word *Bhikkhu* so that the *Ānāpānasati Sutta* reads as follows: *"A mindful parent is somebody who acts in full awareness when going forward and returning . . . ,"* or *"a mindful business leader is somebody who acts in full awareness when walking, standing, sitting, falling asleep, waking up, talking, and keeping silent."*

DIRECT AWARENESS

Direct awareness refers to the insight aspect of mindfulness. It means that there should not be a gap or delay between the experiencing of phenomena and awareness of this experience. In other words, mindfulness is not concerned with the remembering of past events, but involves being intricately aware, in real time, of all present-moment experiences. The term *direct awareness* reminds us that at all times we are deeply and directly connected to all phenomena. This means that when we focus meditative awareness upon the breath, then for all intents and purposes, we become the breath. For the experienced Mindful Warrior, there is no separation between them and the phenomena around them. They breathe in understanding that they are the entire universe, and they breathe out understanding that nothing exists "outside" of themselves.

The direct awareness that we cultivate during authentic mindfulness practice is very penetrating. It looks deeply into phenomena and sees their true and underlying characteristics. The Mindful Warrior understands that all phenomena are subject to impermanence and that they do not exist as isolated or independent entities (we will discuss this in greater detail in chapter 10). By being directly aware of the absolute nature of phenomena, we avoid being deceived by ourselves and other individuals as to the intrinsic value of a particular object, achievement, or situation. In other words, people can try to convince us to buy into the idea of possessing, succeeding, or achieving something, but because we are directly aware of the ultimate mode in which we and all phenomena abide, we are not distracted from walking the path of the Mindful Warrior.

ACTIVE AWARENESS

Active awareness refers to the aspect of mindfulness that encompasses behaving in an ethically wholesome manner. The term *non-*

judgmental is frequently employed in contemporary definitions of mindfulness. However, this term could imply that the mindfulness practitioner is indifferent and doesn't judge which cognitive, emotional, and behavioral responses are ethically appropriate in a given situation. Mindfulness not only involves observing the present moment, but it requires an active participation in it. This is why there is no contradiction in saying that mindfulness features both passive and active elements—the Mindful Warrior is "passively active" in the way they attend to the present moment.

When the Mindful Warrior becomes adept at resting their awareness in the here and now, their thoughts, words, and actions become very powerful. It is accurate to say that everybody's thoughts, words, and actions have far-reaching consequences, but this is particularly the case for an individual who is walking the path of mindful awareness. The Buddha once said that *"Upon a heap of rubbish in the road-side ditch blooms a lotus, fragrant and pleasing. Even so, on the rubbish heap of blinded mortals the disciple of the Supremely Enlightened One shines in resplendent wisdom."*[3] As suggested by these words, it is almost as though by practicing mindfulness and spiritual development, we polish our thoughts, words, and actions such that they begin to shine very brightly. They shed light into the dark corners of people's minds and they become particularly potent in terms of their potential to effect change in the people and environment around us.

By practicing full awareness and active awareness as described above, the Mindful Warrior is deeply aware of what is happening in the present moment. They might not be aware of every single sound or movement in the environment around them, but they are intricately aware of the "feeling" of the present moment and what direction it is moving in. They know if the tide of the present moment is moving in or out, they know the underlying intentions of those with whom they are interacting, and they know how to intervene in such a way that they foster awakening and understanding in the minds and hearts of the people they interact with. As a consequence of being awake to what is happening in the here and now, the Mindful Warrior is able to respond with skill and wisdom. In effect, they learn to dance and play with the present moment, and almost without trying, their basic presence introduces peace and harmony into their surrounding environment.

Thus, the words *active awareness* imply that mindfulness involves making judgments about how to work with what is unfolding in the here and now. They imply that the authentic mindfulness practitioner is somebody who is passionate about the present moment and who actively engages with it. In summary, active awareness means that along with being awake to the present moment comes a tremendous responsibility to respond with kindness, wisdom, and ethical awareness. In truth, all human beings have this responsibility, but because most people do not live and walk in awareness, they do not understand their responsibility.

EXPERIENCED PHENOMENA

Experienced phenomena refers to the "effortless" or "spontaneous" aspect of mindfulness. It means that we should take whatever we happen to be experiencing in the here and now as the object of meditative awareness. In essence, it means that mindfulness is something that we should be practicing and cultivating at all times. As individuals on the path of the Mindful Warrior, we should not be limited by the idea that meditation is something that we engage in at certain times but not at others.

At the moment that experiences arise, we should try to take them onto the path and encompass them within our meditative practice. If the mind is clear and calm, we observe and participate in that experience. But we do exactly the same if the mind is busy and agitated. In other words, we treat all encounters and experiences in the same manner. We begin to experience phenomena as though they are of the same underlying nature and "flavor." Because we are simply observing experience as it unfolds in front of us, it makes no difference whether we are coming or going, winning or losing, busy or at rest. The space from where we observe ourselves and the world around us becomes our permanent place of residence. It is as though we are seated at the center of all universes watching the planets as they move through their cycle of formation, flourishing, and dissolution. It sounds like a strange thing to say, but in a world where everything is impermanent, we begin to experience a degree of permanence. We are permanently experiencing the impermanence around us. This is a very liberating experience.

SPIRITUAL IN ASPECT

Spiritual in aspect refers to the "compassionate" and "transpersonal" aspects of mindfulness. In essence, it means that the primary intention for practicing mindfulness is to effect spiritual awakening in oneself and others. It is this underlying intention that helps to distinguish mindfulness from (for example) an attention-based psychological technique designed to improve concentration, cognitive functioning, and/or levels of psychosomatic wellbeing. In other words, "spiritual in aspect" implies that the Mindful Warrior engages in mindfulness practice in order to completely and permanently overcome suffering. It implies that they understand that there exists, within their own being, the capacity to awaken to enlightened wisdom, omniscience, and unconditional compassion. The term *spiritual in aspect* means that the Mindful Warrior's commitment to the practice of mindfulness is unyielding and stems from an understanding that self, birth, death, and ignorance are all concepts that can be transcended.

As part of using mindfulness techniques within applied settings, it seems that some mindfulness teachers are reluctant to use the word *spiritual* in their description of the practice. Presumably, their reasoning for not doing this is because they believe that organizations and members of the public assign negative connotations to this word. However, in some instances and while avoiding using the term *spiritual*, the same individuals describe the mindful techniques they are teaching as being embodiments of the Buddhist Dharma. *Dharma* is a Sanskrit word, and in the context referred to here, it means Buddhist teachings. So, on the one hand, some mindfulness teachers are informing people that their techniques are not spiritual, but on the other hand, they are claiming to teach a technique that embodies the Buddhist teachings.[4] In our opinion, this is a very confusing and misleading message to put across.

If it is the case that contemporary mindfulness techniques truly happen to embody the Buddhist *Dharma*, then by default, they are spiritual in nature. Consequently, we believe that the best approach is to be transparent and honest with people. If something is spiritual, then let's call it spiritual. We don't need to be frightened of using this word. Research studies are increasingly showing that there are health benefits associated with practicing mindfulness. If it can be demonstrated that spiritual approaches—such as mindfulness—are supported by empirical evidence, then people will become more comfortable with using the word *spiritual* and with engaging in spiritual activities. However, if researchers and scientists veer away from describing mindfulness and other types of evidence-based meditation practice as spiritual, then *spiritual* will remain a taboo word.

It makes us sad when people try to ignore or forget that they have a spiritual side to their being. Spirituality is a part of who and what we are. Whether we like it or not, and whether we know it or not, everything that we do is a spiritual act. Our thoughts, words, and actions influence the long-term happiness of every other sentient being and all phenomena in the universe. They influence who we are now and who we will be in the future. When we observe ourselves living and participating in the present moment, and when we are mindful of how we interact with the world, these are spiritual acts. The Mindful Warrior knows this and is not afraid to call themselves a spiritual person, or to call mindfulness a spiritual practice.

MAINTAINED FROM ONE MOMENT TO THE NEXT

Maintained from one moment to the next refers to the enduring aspect of mindfulness. It means that the Mindful Warrior should aim to maintain an unbroken flow of awareness throughout the day and night. The Buddha once said that just like a fire that smokes and cinders at night after burning during the day, the level of calm and awareness experienced by the mind when we are asleep is heavily influenced by the level of calm and awareness that we experience during waking hours. In other words, if we are stressed and agitated during the day, the likelihood is that we will be stressed and agitated when dreaming and during sleep. Conversely, if we manage to cultivate a good level of meditative tranquility and awareness during the day, this awareness tends to stay with us when we are asleep. In fact, there are reports of some very experienced Buddhist meditation practitioners who have been able to maintain full meditative awareness while dreaming (which should not be confused with the notion of lucid dreaming in Western psychology).

There are certain meditative techniques that can be employed to try to induce meditative dreaming. However, we don't need to concern ourselves with these for the time being. Rather, we should focus on maintaining meditative awareness throughout the day and allowing this awareness to spill over into sleep in as natural a manner as possible. We can facilitate this spill-over process by practicing meditation immediately before going to bed and by trying to maintain meditative awareness as we enter sleep.

Each night before getting into bed, consider taking some time to be on your own. Sit on a chair in the bedroom or on the side of the bed, and take ten minutes to attend to your breathing. Try not to think about the day that has passed or what awaits you tomorrow. Just sit in a relaxed but stable posture and enjoy being present with yourself. When you are ready and while maintaining mindful awareness, gently slip under the bedcovers and assume whatever posture is most comfortable for sleep. Continue to observe your breath as it flows in and out. Observe the lungs as they rise and fall. Notice any feelings of tiredness in the body but at the same time, become aware of the feeling of contentment that arises because the body can take a rest. Breathe in and feel calm, and breathe out and feel content. After you have spent a few minutes cradling the body in awareness, try to become aware of your thoughts. Observe how they suddenly appear in the mind, sometimes without any link to the last thought. However, remember not to feed or hold onto your thoughts. Just allow them to flicker through the mind-space. In this manner, thoughts begin to behave like a shooting star—beautiful occurrences that arise and dissolve in the briefest moment of time. If you can observe your thoughts—one after the other—it means your practice is progressing nicely, and we are sure that you will enjoy a peaceful night's sleep.

AUTHENTIC MINDFULNESS

By encompassing each of the above aspects of mindfulness into our day-to-day practice, we will develop into strong meditation practitioners. There will be no danger of us becoming distracted by trivial concerns and falling away from the path that leads to freedom and transcendent wisdom. At the moment, there is a lot of hype surrounding mindfulness and lots of people are expressing an interest in it. However, without understanding its profundity and the various aspects that make mindfulness complete and effective, many people will reach a point where they begin to wonder what all the hype was about. They will become bored with mindfulness and will start to look for the next quick-fix solution.

The difference between the Mindful Warrior and other mindfulness practitioners is that the Mindful Warrior is absolutely sincere in the way they embody and practice mindfulness. They are absolutely rooted in the present moment and in the knowledge that they are an aspiring enlightened being. The Mindful Warrior doesn't care if mindfulness is popular or unpopular, and they are not deceived by charismatic words. They are intricately and experientially aware of the subtle aspects of mindfulness. They are resolute in their practice. They live their practice. The Mindful Warrior is 100 percent here and 100 percent now.

A CLOSE TRUTH

We would like to finish this chapter with a vajragiti that we wrote called "A Close Truth." The vajragiti refers to some of the subtler aspects of mindfulness and spiritual practice. If we practice mindfulness in order get somewhere or attain something, this is very self-oriented and it will prevent us from seeing the truth that is directly in front of our eyes. However, if we approach mindfulness with a selfless attitude, look deeply into the present moment, and make it our home, then it won't be long before the present moment reveals its true colors.

> *Like the repose that follows,*
> *When waking from a nightmare.*
> *Like the reprieve of an isolated General,*
> *Who recognizes the encroaching soldiers as his own troops.*
> *Like the relief that arises, when realizing that the snake,*
> *Was, all along, just a piece of old rope.*
> *Like the rapture of the despairing treasure hunter,*
> *Who returns to find the riches buried beneath their own home.*
> *Oh self who has enslaved me for so long,*
> *Now I have shed the shackles of ignorance,*
> *And entered the non-returning blissful abode.*

6

A STICKY MIND

Have you ever engaged in an activity so much that when you close your eyes, you still see images relating to what you were doing? An example might be if you have spent the whole day at the beach watching the waves, and then when you close your eyes just before going to sleep, you see waves moving through your mind. The mind is a very powerful creature that, as we will go on to discuss in this chapter, has the tendency to absorb its external environment. In fact, the more we expose ourselves to particular environmental, psychological, and spiritual stimuli, the more the mind begins to assimilate the basic "energy" of these stimuli. This is why the Buddhist teachings advise that we should take care, when possible, in choosing our friends, livelihood, and place of residence. For example, in a key Buddhist text known as the Dhammapada, the Buddha is recorded to have taught that *"should a seeker not find a companion who is better or equal, let him resolutely pursue a solitary course; there is no fellowship with the fool."*[1]

It is common knowledge (and common sense) that the way the mind develops is influenced by the type of stimuli and conditions it is exposed to. This is the basic principle that underlies the notions of "classical" and "operant" conditioning in contemporary psychology. In the case of classical conditioning, an involuntary behavioral response (such as feeling hungry) is triggered by a particular stimulus (such as catching a smell of food being cooked in the oven). In the case of operant conditioning, a particular stimulus (such as feeling hungry) triggers a voluntary behavioral response (such as cooking something to eat). It is also well known in psychology that the types of environmental, social, and psychological conditions a person is exposed to during childhood and adolescence significantly influence their risk of developing a mental health problem later in life. However, the absorbing quality of the mind that we wish to refer to and discuss in this chapter is much more immediate and direct than how contemporary psychology understands and teaches this subject.

Contemporary psychology accepts that a person's mind and behavior is conditioned by the environmental and psychological stimuli that they encounter. But what we are suggesting is that the mind is not only conditioned by its external environment, but it actually "absorbs" its external environment. Perhaps the closest notion in contemporary psychology to the quality of mind that we are talking about is Game Transfer Phenomena.[2] This is a condition experienced by some frequent video-game players who exhibit signs of game play during their downtime (i.e., when they are engaged in other activities). Typical symptoms include automatic motor activations (such as involuntary impulses and reflexes), intrusive game-related thoughts, and certain pseudo-hallucinatory experiences such as optical illusions.

What we are proposing, and what scientific research such as this appears to support, is that the mind, even in adulthood, is "sticky." It's as though every single thing we do and experience leaves an imprint or shadow on the mind. Depending upon how often we relive that experience (whether through actually repeating it or just through thinking about it), the imprint either becomes much more pronounced, or it begins to fade away (but without ever fully disappearing). Certain events in our life make a huge impression on the mind and firmly imprint on it after just a single exposure. An example might be a single traumatic experience that individuals relive (and therefore psychologically reinforce) for many years after the event. Other events and experiences, such as digesting and listening to spiritual teachings, might require a greater deal of exposure over a longer period of time before they eventually form strong imprints upon the mind.

As we move through life, the sticky or absorbing property of the mind means that we end up with an incredibly large number of mental imprints. Depending upon whether we experienced the situations that helped to form these imprints as pleasing or unpleasing, the imprints cause us to develop attachments or aversions to particular situations, objects, and energy. For example, if there was a time in our lives when we experienced a sense of excitement, companionship, and escapism while drinking alcohol with friends, we might develop an attachment to this experience and seek to repeat it as often as possible. Alternatively, if drinking alcohol with friends has not been a pleasant experience for us, then it is possible that we will develop an aversion to this experience and prefer not to engage in social encounters of this nature.

Becoming acquainted with the process of how imprints form on the mind, and the mind's absorbing and sticky quality more generally, is key to understanding the nature of suffering. Suffering is a condition of human existence. Because we are born, we suffer. However, if we understand clearly why suffering arises, then we can start to change our relationship with suffering and use it as a tool for promoting psychological and spiritual growth. In fact, the extent to which a person is able to understand and work with suffering is perhaps the single biggest factor that determines how quickly they progress along the path of mindful warriorship.

THE NATURE OF SUFFERING

Suffering, like all things, is produced by causes. If you burn your finger on a hot pan, there are numerous factors that play a causal role. The hot pan is one factor and the gas flame that caused it to heat up is another factor. The fact that you pay the gas bill on time is a further factor, and if you were feeling a little tired or distracted, then this might also have contributed. Each of these causes (of which there are many more) are themselves the effect of other causes. For example, assuming that you used natural gas as your source of fuel for heating the pan, then there must exist the technology to identify, extract, and process the gas from reserves buried deep beneath the surface of the earth.

The same principle applies to suffering that is more psychological in nature. If we are feeling particularly anxious or low, there are many factors that have caused these feelings to arise. We could spend a long time trying to trace all of these factors, and it is possible that doing so would lead us back to circumstances that we were exposed to early on in life. It is certainly a good exercise to try to identify all the various factors that play a role in the onset of a particular course of suffering. However, in truth, this can be a difficult exercise to perform because the sheer number of contributing causes means that it is hard to pinpoint them all. Consequently, a far more productive and effective method is to identify and target the underlying cause of all forms of suffering. If we manage to establish what the root cause of all forms of suffering is, then all we have to do is dismantle this cause and we will cease to experience suffering.

In order for suffering to arise, there needs to be a self that experiences it. For example, suffering isn't experienced by a mountain or a cloud. A cloud doesn't experience suffering because it knows that it doesn't exist as an independent self. The cloud knows that it exists only in reliance upon (for example) the wind, rivers, oceans, sun, and mountains. The cloud understands that it is a manifestation of all these contributing factors. In essence, the cloud does not exist in and of itself. It manifests in reliance upon causes and conditions, and if any of these are not present, the cloud ceases to exist.

Harboring the belief that we intrinsically exist (i.e., independently of all other things) is the primary underlying cause of suffering. Where there exists a self, there exists suffering. And where there exists suffering, there exists a self. Imagine that you experience suffering in the form of anger because a person has just reversed into your brand-new car. Looking to the causes of the feeling of anger, it is easy to point the finger at the other person and place the blame on them. As far as the car accident is concerned, it may well be that the other person is completely at fault. But it is not their fault that you become angry.

The anger that arises in a scenario such as this is of our own making. The primary underlying factor that causes us to become angry is the fact that we are caught up in the idea of a "me," a "mine," and an "I." We believe that we are a self that intrinsically exists and that the car is something that belongs to this self. We become angry because we think that as a result of the accident, the self is going to lose out. We might be angry because we know that the car accident will cost us money and time on repairs. However, probably the biggest reason we feel angry is because the car no longer looks new and beautiful and we feel its image reflects poorly on us.

As indicated by the example above, suffering is all about the ego. If we remove the ego from the equation, then there is no longer a reason for us to become angry. Without the ego, it is much easier to understand that having a minor car accident is not really a big deal. There are many millions of people driving quickly on congested roads in big metal boxes on wheels. It is therefore inevitable that from time to time they are going to hit each other, and that when they do one or both vehicles will be damaged. Assuming that nobody is seriously injured in the accident, the situation can be dealt with straightforwardly, and without the need for negative emotions. All we have to do is exchange insurance details, inform our insurance company, and arrange for the car to be repaired.

Without the involvement of the ego, there is no self to be hurt or offended. The incident is not an episode in a continuing soap opera. In fact, without the involvement of the ego, it is actually possible to enjoy situations like this. Instead of wasting time by arguing, we can help to create a present moment that fosters peace and wisdom in ourselves and the other person. We can use the situation as our greatest teacher, and as an opportunity to practice letting go and responding with calm. We let go of our attachment to the car, but more importantly, we let go of our attachment to ourselves.

PLANETS AND STARS IN THE MIND

It sounds obvious that suffering requires a self, and that extinguishing our belief in selfhood will end our suffering. However, as true as this statement may be, it is one thing coming to a conceptual understanding of this principle, but is an entirely different kettle of fish being able to permanently remove our attachment to a me, mine, and I. Since the moment we were born (and from well before this if you subscribe to the view of reincarnation), we have been continuously reinforcing our belief in a self that exists independently of all other things. Although we might rationally understand that the existence of an intrinsic self is logically and scientifically implausible because all things are interconnected, this doesn't stop us from constantly feeding our belief in selfhood. In fact, according to Buddhist meditation literature, everything we think, say, and do—no matter how small or insignificant it may seem—is driven and controlled by the ego.

Imagine that the mind is like a vast expanse of empty space. As we experience thoughts, feelings, and perceptions, this empty space begins to fill up with planets, stars, and other celestial bodies. With each new thought and experience, a star is born in the mind. The star shines brighter or dimmer depending upon how much we think about or relive the experience. In this analogy, these stars and planets are equivalent to the mental imprints that we referred to earlier, and the ego is like an astronaut traveling between them. The astronaut decides that certain planets are beautiful and welcoming, whereas others are ugly, with a harsh environment.

The astronaut constructs a reality with themselves at the center, and everything else peripheral. If the astronaut deems a particular celestial body to be valuable and pleasing, they are drawn to it. Likewise, wherever the astronaut assigns a negative value to a planet or star, they do their best to avoid it. Although, from the ego's point of view, relating to the world in this manner makes a lot of sense, it offers the ego a very limited perspective on reality. Through the porthole of their spaceship, the astronaut only ever gets a partial picture of what is happening.

The ego's preferred approach is to avoid what it doesn't like and focus on the people, objects, and circumstances that it is attracted to. However, this strategy is destined to fail because in addition to not having complete control over what happens in our external environment, our preferences and desires are also continuously changing. For example, a person might decide that living in the city is far too claustrophobic. Consequently, they move to the countryside in order to enjoy a slower pace of life and to spend more time with nature, their family, and themselves. However, after a few years, they start to get bored (including with themselves) and to miss the conveniences and lifestyle of city living. In other words, whether it's their place of residence, job, car, or partner, after a short "honeymoon" period of so-called happiness, people have a tendency to be dissatisfied with their lot.

Our suffering has absolutely nothing to do with the fact that imprints are constantly forming in the mind. Absorbency is a natural quality of the mind and so it is inevitable that the mind assimilates the various phenomena and situations that it encounters. Rather, suffering arises because we form all kinds of complicated relationships with these mental imprints, and we become attached or averse to them as well as the phenomena and situations that created them. Instead of accepting and experiencing environmental and psychological phenomena "as they are," we always have to make them about the me, the mine, and the I. During each moment of the day, we are in contact with many beautiful things, but because we are always creating soap operas in our mind and in other people's minds, we are unable to experience this beauty.

If the astronaut stopped conceptually adding to and subtracting from the celestial bodies they encountered, their viewing window would become much bigger. They would find themselves in a spaceship made entirely of glass, and from which they could enjoy a 360-degree perspective. In fact, as we become more adept at using meditation in order to undermine the ego, the walls of the spaceship eventually begin to break down altogether. There reaches a point where there is no longer a barrier separating us from the impressions that have formed in the mind. Having no protective layer might sound like a daunting prospect, but by realizing that these impressions have no substance and are nothing more than our own mental projections, we come to realize that there isn't—and never has been—anything to fear.

DISSOLVING THE EGO

Without an ego to scrutinize, conceptualize, and categorize the various psychological and environmental phenomena that we encounter, what was once experienced as many starts to become whole again. The vast majority of people view reality through the lens of an ego that deems itself separate from all of their mental imprints, as well as the situations and experiences that caused these imprints to develop. In other words, most people separate existence into: (i) the observing ego or self, (ii) the internal psychological world, and (iii) the external physical world. However, by allowing the ego to dissolve into the empty space and universe around them, the Mindful Warrior no longer makes such divisions. They experience all aspects of reality as one thing, and do not think in terms of an ego-self that observes and is separate from its inner or outer world.

Can you recall the guided meditation that was included at the end of chapter 1? This meditation comprised ten exercises, and the eighth exercise was as follows: *Breathing in, I am aware of the space and time that exists between my in-breath and out-breath, and between my out-breath and in-breath; breathing out, I relax into this space and time*. We can use meditative breathing to access and better understand the principle that we are discussing in this chapter of the internal and external world dissolving into one.

When we focus awareness on the gap between the in-breath and out-breath, the gap starts to expand. With practice, it is possible to reach a point where time seems to come to a stop, and where we move beyond the notion of breathing in and out. In this gap, which also exists between the appearance of one thought and another, we can experience life without concepts and boundaries.

Due to not compartmentalizing reality, the accomplished Mindful Warrior is without a me, mine, or I that can be insulted, hurt, or offended. Suffering requires something to happen in our psychological or physical environment that in some way threatens the existence or ideals of the ego-self. However, if there is no longer an ego that can consider itself poorly treated, then suffering cannot arise. Learning to see the world without the interference of the ego is at the heart of mindfulness practice. Mindfulness means that we understand that the mind is complete and is full of absolutely everything. In a mind that is complete and encompasses everything, suffering is unable to take hold.

If the ocean decides that it doesn't like a particular wave, or if a wave decides that it doesn't like the ocean, this is a maladaptive way of perceiving reality. If the ocean has a gripe with a wave, it means that the ocean has a gripe with itself. Likewise, if a wave has a gripe with the ocean, it means that the wave has a gripe with itself. However, when the wave and ocean consider themselves to be manifestations of a single whole, there is no longer any basis for conflict to arise. The wave is inseparable from the ocean, just as we are everything that we experience, and everything that we experience—including that which we deem to be suffering—is us. Mindfulness allows us to see the mind as whole and complete, and to once again experience the beauty that is all around us.

In this chapter we have used the analogy of the mind as a vast expanse of empty space, and seeing thoughts and resultant mental imprints as planets and stars. This may seem like a strange way to think about the mind and reality but believe it or not, this analogy is not as far from the truth as you might think. With every single thought, we create a new world. Each and every thought that we have changes the trajectory of the present moment and resets the future. The raw material of which thoughts are made is incredibly powerful. Thoughts, in essence, are made of pure creative energy. They are made of the same basic energy that sparked the big bang. How wonderful!

BECAUSE I THINK I AM

We would like to conclude this chapter on suffering with a short reflection that we wrote called "Because I Think I Am." This reflection refers to an individual's changing relationship with suffering as they progress along the path of the Mindful Warrior.

> *Because I think I am, I want to be.*
> *Because I want to be, I want to possess.*
> *Because I want to possess, I suffer.*
> *Because I suffer, I want to suffer less.*
> *Because I want to suffer less, I suffer more.*
> *Because I suffer more, I stop trying to possess.*
> *Because I stop trying to possess, I experience life as a whole.*
> *Because I experience life as a whole, I no longer need to be.*
> *Because I no longer need to be, I truly am.*

7

THE COMPASSIONATE HEART

Compassion is the glue that holds humanity together. It doesn't matter if we are talking about the relationship between two individuals in a family or the relationship between two countries, if people are not kind and caring toward each other, things deteriorate very quickly. In fact, history shows that when fear, ignorance, and selfishness prevail over compassion and loving-kindness, there is often no point of 'bottoming-out' in terms of the negativity that ensues. Hatred, anger, and violence invariably foster more negative emotions, and minor disagreements can quickly escalate into global conflict.

Although the cultivation of compassion and loving-kindness is concerned with fostering harmony in our relationships with other people and in the environment around us, it is also concerned with fostering harmony within ourselves. There is the old adage that when we give, we also receive. In this respect, cultivating compassion and loving-kindness represents a win-win scenario. Not only does our kindness benefit others, but we, as the donor of kindness, also receive immense benefit.

In the traditional Buddhist literature, loving-kindness and compassion are two of the Four Sublime Attitudes (Sanskrit: *brahmaviharahs*)—the other two being sympathetic joy and equanimity. Sympathetic joy highlights the fact that authentic loving-kindness and compassion can only manifest in a mind that is unconditionally joyful and that is in continuous contact with meditative tranquility. 'Equanimity' emphasizes the need for the cultivation of loving-kindness and compassion to be extended in equal and unlimited measure to all living beings (i.e., irrespective of whether we consider them to be a friend or an enemy). Therefore, any discussion of how loving-kindness and compassion help us to mature as Mindful Warriors needs to consider how these practices relate to, and are supported by, joy and equanimity.

In chapter 3, we discussed how paying attention to detail (while not getting caught up in it), fearlessness, joyfulness, and being a humble servant of humanity, each form part of the Mindful Warrior's code of practice. In this chapter, we explore the code of practice of the Mindful Warrior a little further and focus specifically on cultivating love, kindness, and a compassionate heart. As part of this discussion, we make reference to what we call the "close" and "distant" enemies of loving-kindness and compassion (as well as the "close" and "distant" enemies of the related spiritual practices of joy and equanimity). The term *close enemy* refers to methods of spiritual practice that, on the surface, appear to be similar to authentic loving-kindness and compassion but actually have no place on the path of the Mindful Warrior. The term *distant enemy* refers to behaviors and states of mind that directly undermine the development of a loving and compassionate heart.

LOVING-KINDNESS

In the meditation literature, loving-kindness is often defined as the wish for all beings to have happiness and its causes. This doesn't mean that as aspiring Mindful Warriors we single-handedly have to save the world or end poverty in developing nations. If this were the case, then we would have to conclude that all of the great spiritual leaders such as Christ and the Buddha failed in their roles. Rather, cultivating and practicing loving-kindness means that we should engender the wish, from deep within our being, for happiness and peace to spread throughout the world. This isn't a wish that we take up from time to time and then forget about. It is an intention that we cultivate and strive to carry with us during every moment of our lives.

A single candle can light a thousand candles, and each of these can light a thousand more. The practice of loving-kindness is basically concerned with lighting a candle of kindness, warmth, and wisdom within ourselves, and allowing the light from this candle to steadily grow stronger, and touch increasingly more living beings. A mind that is imbued with loving-kindness effortlessly emanates happiness and warmth, and the ripple from this positive energy can spread across the globe.

Research shows that practicing loving-kindness leads to increases in positive emotions and that these, in turn, foster richer interpersonal relationships, increased sense of purpose, improvements in quality of life, and a decrease in both bodily pain and psychological issues such as depression, anxiety, and distress.[1] The collective evidence from loving-kindness research studies demonstrates that the extent to which we manage to cultivate loving-kindness in our hearts and minds significantly influences how we think, feel, and act toward a particular person or situation (including how we think, feel, and act toward ourselves).

For example, depending upon whether we are feeling kind toward ourselves and others in a particular moment of time, a neutral comment from our boss might be interpreted in many different ways. If we happen to go to work with a closed, negative, and selfish mind, and the boss asks us for a simple explanation as to why something went wrong, we might automatically presume that they are implying that we are at fault. The normal immediate reaction in such a situation would probably be for feelings of anger and worry to begin to well up in our mind and stomach. We might think that the boss has it in for us and we might say things that we later regret. However, if we are feeling settled and solid in ourselves and loving toward others, we are more likely to see that our boss is (hopefully) just doing their job and asking a valid question.

We can respond to it confidently and then move on and enjoy the rest of our day without giving the matter further thought.

In the *Dhammapada*,[2] the Buddha is recorded to have said:

> All we experience is preceded by mind,
> Led by mind, made by mind.
> Speak or act with a corrupt mind
> And suffering follows
> As the wagon wheel follows the hoof of the ox.
>
> All we experience is preceded by mind,
> Led by mind, made by mind.
> Speak or act with a peaceful mind
> And happiness follows
> Like a shadow that never leaves.

The words *"all we experience is preceded by the mind"* are very profound and capture the essence of Buddhism. Rather than being reliant upon external factors, happiness is ultimately a choice that we make. If we wish to experience unconditional happiness, we should focus all our efforts on training the mind, and on changing how it relates to and experiences the world. At the beginning, this isn't a particularly easy thing to do, but equally it isn't a tremendously difficult thing to do. It's a case of getting started and remaining resolute. If we do this, then it won't be too long before our efforts start to bear fruit.

We once conducted a randomized controlled trial in which middle managers working in office-based roles received training in meditation. At the start of the training program, most participants were under the impression that the only way to tangibly improve their levels of job satisfaction would be to change jobs or for their employer to make certain changes to human resource management systems such as improving flexibility in working hours, increasing their salary, or introducing better rewards programs. However, after completing the eight-week Meditation Awareness Training program that focused on changing employees' internal psychological environment rather than their external work environment, participants experienced significant improvements in job satisfaction (as well as psychological wellbeing and job perfor-mance).[3]

Of course, there are certainly things that employers can do to make the working environment more stimulating and accommo-dating of people's needs, but in our opinion, employers and em-ployees both often underestimate the benefits that can be derived by using carefully designed contemplative interventions.

The Enemies of Loving-Kindness

The close enemy of loving-kindness is showing selfish affection toward others. If we do something that is kind with the intention of being patted on the back, then this is a distorted form of loving-kindness. Some people like to hear words such as "Oh, what a kind person you are" or "What a lovely gesture—you are so kind." However, as individuals on the path of the Mindful Warrior, we are not really interested in being praised or recognized for our actions. Loving-kindness is just a part of who we are. It's what we do. If people choose to praise us, that's good, but we are not seeking praise.

Authentic loving-kindness is completely unconditional; it en-compasses all living beings irrespective of whether they "deserve" it. Loving-kindness is given freely and without any expectation of a return. It is said that loving-kindness is actually the basis upon which compassion should be constructed because in order to feel empathy with those who are suffering (including ourselves), we must truly—and with all of our hearts—wish for the wellbeing of others.

The distant enemy of loving-kindness is hatred or ill-will. There is no room for hatred on the path of the Mindful Warrior. If a person has hatred for others, it means they have hatred for them-selves. Sometimes in the news you read about a person who has been unkind to animals receiving threats of violence (or even threats of death) from people who supposedly love animals and who seek revenge. However, this is just an example of ill-will and hatred fostering even more ill-will and hatred. When hatred is allowed to grow in the mind, it can quickly undo a lifetime's worth of spiritual practice.

Cultivating Loving-Kindness

The first step is to foster loving-kindness toward ourselves. When we have unconditional love for our own being, then all our thoughts, words, and actions become an expression of that love. Until we resolve the conflict within ourselves, we are not in a strong position to resolve the conflict and problems that exist in the world around us. If we try to convince others to live peacefully and responsibly when we have tension and conflict in our own hearts, then despite our best intentions, we are just going to create more suffering and confusion.

The end goal is for loving-kindness to become our normal, natural, and spontaneous way of being. However, until that happens (and it will sooner or later), we have to rely on specific practices and techniques in order to break maladaptive thinking and behavioral patterns. A useful practice in this respect involves the repetition, during meditation, of particular phrases. The following is an example of a meditation that can be practiced in order to cultivate loving-kindness for both ourselves and others. While practicing this meditation, you can either verbalize the phrases, or if wished, you can just mentally repeat them:

> As I breathe in, I feel peace infuse my body and mind;
> As I breathe out, I relax and feel well in my body and mind.
> As I breathe in, I sense a calm happiness growing inside me;
> As I breathe out, I relax and bathe in this happiness.
> As I breathe in, I remember that I am alive in the here and now;
> As I breathe out, I smile gently toward myself.
> As I breathe in, I collect feelings of happiness into my heart;
> As I breathe out, I direct this happiness deep into my being.
> As I breathe in, I feel awake and alive;
> As I breathe out, I feel nourished and revitalized.

When practicing this meditation, we can, from time to time, change the wording; for example, the part that says, *"As I breathe out, I direct this happiness deep into my being"* to *"As I breathe out, I direct this happiness deep into the hearts and minds of other people."* In addition to people in general, we can also choose specific individuals to be the recipient of our feelings of loving-kindness. For example, we could say, *"As I breathe out, I direct this happiness deep into the heart and mind of my dear friend Carol"* or *"As I breathe out, I direct this happiness deep into the heart and mind of the office bully who causes me to suffer when I am at work."* We can also direct feelings of loving-kindness toward situations that we may or may not be personally involved with. For example, *"As I breathe out, I direct this happiness deep into the hearts and minds of my brothers and sisters who are experiencing famine and disease in Zimbabwe"* or *"As I breathe out, I direct this happiness deep into the hearts and minds of all the people who, like me, are brave enough to leave behind soap opera living and embark on the path of the Mindful Warrior."* We can sit in formal meditation posture to practice this meditation, but we can also practice it when we are (for example) traveling in the car, working at the computer, or eating lunch at work.

COMPASSION

Compassion is often defined as the wish for all living beings to be free from suffering and its causes. This wish is basically what is implied by the Sanskrit word *Bodhicitta* (which means the "mind of awakening"). *Bodhicitta* refers to an attitude or motivation to undertake spiritual practice for the primary purpose of benefitting others. In Buddhism, people who adopt and act upon such an attitude are known as *bodhisattvas*. The Mindful Warrior could be thought of as a *bodhisattva* who dedicates their life toward alleviating ignorance and suffering within both themselves and others.

In order to cultivate compassion effectively, we need to fully understand the nature of suffering. We need to understand the various attributes of suffering that we discussed in chapter 6, and the fact that irrespective of whether they are consciously aware of it, all living beings are immersed in suffering. However, we also need to understand that if suffering did not exist, it would not be possible to cultivate compassion. Without the possibility of cultivating compassion, it would not be possible to make rapid spiritual progress and take our rightful place at the side of the accomplished Mindful Warriors who have walked this path before us.

When we see an animal or a person in distress and pain, it is possible that we might desperately wish to alleviate their suffering and bring them some peace and tranquility. It is wonderful when a person (or animal) is moved by, and takes action to lighten the suffering of another living being. This is an example of compassion at its most raw and basic level. However, as we grow in awareness and wisdom as Mindful Warriors, we start to see that even when people are not openly displaying signs of distress, they are still subject to suffering. Consequently, authentic compassion requires great wisdom and skill. Wisdom is required to cut through the façade of superficial happiness that people often choose to hide behind. Skill is required to know how best to help people who may be reluctant to change their ways.

In addition to loving-kindness, scientists are also becoming increasingly interested in the attributes, correlates, and applications of compassion. Research shows that compassion meditation gives rise to various health benefits as well as more adaptive psychosocial functioning. For example, the regular practice of compassion meditation has been shown to reduce levels of a biological marker known as C-reactive protein. High levels of C-reactive protein indicate that there is inflammation in the body, which is often a sign that there is an underlying health problem. Compassion meditation has also been shown to increase activity in brain areas that help us to regulate emotions, including those associated with low and depressive mood states.

When we have profound compassion for our own and others' suffering and pain, we begin to see the world and people around us very differently. By bringing the needs and suffering of others into our field of awareness, we are better able to add perspective to our own problems and suffering. We become less self-obsessed and more allocentric or "other-centered," and the positive thinking patterns that underlie this newfound perspective help us to feel vibrant, confident, and alive. Compassion prevents us from experiencing life as a constant struggle and from getting caught up with what we deem to be our problems.

In fact, not only do we begin to see the world differently when we practice compassion, but the world begins to see us differently. As we begin to understand how to act skillfully and compassionately in any given situation, the present moment and the phenomena that it contains begin to talk to us. A compassionate mind is an open mind, it perceives new sounds, smells, tastes, and sights, and it is able to tune into the heartbeat of the here and now. When unconditional compassion has flowered in the mind, the earth relaxes and breathes out a huge sigh of relief. Amid all of the chaos, mindlessness, and exploitation of natural resources, the earth has a new friend and guardian—a child of the Mindful Warriors who walks gently and gracefully upon her shoulders.

The Enemies of Compassion

The close enemy of compassion is pity. If we walk past a homeless person in the street, we might experience a feeling of empathy. We might even be inspired to give them some money or to make a donation to a charitable organization. However, how much of this donation is to do with actually helping the person and how much is to do with our own feelings of guilt? Pity is a distorted form of compassion that is self-focused. If we wish to make a donation to a homeless person, then we should do so with confidence and kindness, and without feelings of guilt. We should make the donation with a good understanding of how the money is likely to be spent, and whether the individual will put it to good use. We should consider the option of providing the individual with the other resources they need (including friendship and support) in order to make more lasting improvements to their situation.

Compassion's distant enemy is cruelty. We can be cruel with our thoughts just as much as we can be cruel with our words and actions. Acts of cruelty cause other people to suffer but they also cause the perpetrator to suffer. The perpetrator of cruelty suffers guilt and self-hatred. Being cruel doesn't necessarily have to involve doing something, because not doing something can also constitute an act of cruelty. For example, people who have the opportunity to follow a path of authentic spiritual teachings but choose to remain in soap opera living are arguably being cruel toward themselves, as well as toward others.

Cultivating Compassion

There are many ways to cultivate and practice compassion. However, if we want a particular wholesome attitude to work its way deep into our being, then meditation is a very effective and direct method. The mental space, clarity, and calm that we cultivate during meditation allows us to rapidly cultivate and assimilate wholesome psychological and spiritual qualities. During meditation, we plant seeds of compassion deep within our being, and we water these seeds as we interact with the living beings and phenomena around us.

As with most of the skills that the Mindful Warrior needs to develop, we should start by cultivating compassion for ourselves, and then gradually begin to direct this compassionate energy toward others. The following is a meditation that can be used to help us do this. The first part of the meditation is concerned with developing meditative focus and calm, and the second part focuses on the cultivation of compassion for one's own suffering. It's really up to you how long you take to practice this meditation, but we would suggest a few minutes on each in- and out-breath exercise.

As I breathe in, I observe myself breathing in;
As I breathe out, I observe myself breathing out.

As I breathe in, I know whether my breath is deep or shallow, short or long;
As I breathe out, I allow my breath to follow its natural course.
As I breathe in, I observe the space and time that exists between my in-breath and out-breath;
As I breathe out, I relax into this space and time.
As I breathe in, I understand that there is nowhere else I need to be;
As I breathe out, I understand that I am already at home.
As I breathe in, I am aware of the suffering that is present inside of me;
As I breathe out, I cradle my suffering in meditative awareness.
As I breathe in, I observe difficult feelings and thoughts that are moving within my mind;
As I breathe out, I allow those feelings and thoughts to calm and relax.
As I breathe in, I understand that suffering is born of causes and conditions;
As I breathe out, I understand that suffering does not exist as a standalone entity.
As I breathe in, I collect my suffering into a sphere of energy located in my heart;
As I breathe out, I allow my suffering to dissolve into the universe around me.
As I breathe in, I allow joy and happiness to gather in a sphere of energy located in my heart;
As I breathe out, I bathe in those feelings of joy and happiness.
As I breathe in, I understand that other people also suffer;
As I breathe out, I radiate feelings of joy and happiness to others.
As I breathe in, I return to simply following my breathing;
As I breathe out, I enjoy the experience of simply being.

The above meditation mostly focuses on raising awareness of the suffering present inside of us, and on transforming that suffering into happiness and joyful energy. However, after repeated practice, you might reach the point where you feel ready and able to give greater consideration to the suffering of others. When this happens, you can change the words to reflect your growing wish to reach out to other people. For example, you could change the words to *"As I breathe in, I collect the suffering of others into a sphere of energy located in my heart; as I breathe out, I allow this suffering to be carried by my out-breath and to dissolve into the air and universe around me."* In much the same manner as we outlined when discussing the cultivation of loving-kindness, you can take the suffering of people in general as the object of your meditation, or you can choose a particular individual or situation.

An important consideration concerning the practice of compassion meditation is not to start feeling weighed down by your or other people's suffering. In fact, the reason we recommend that you collect and "process" suffering in a sphere (or a ball) of energy at the center of your heart, is to help you objectify and remain separate from suffering. If we get too involved with our and others' suffering and don't know how to relate to it correctly, we risk developing a condition known as "compassion fatigue" or "empathy burnout." This condition is most frequently associated with individuals working in frontline health care roles such as nurses, doctors, emergency responders, and mental health professionals. The symptoms can include chronic stress, anxiety, apathy, destructive thinking patterns, and insomnia. Thus, from a certain point of view, we could say that caring too much can actually be detrimental to our own health. It is for this exact reason (i.e., to avoid the risk of becoming a victim of their own compassion) that it is essential that the Mindful Warrior develops discriminating wisdom and—as we will discuss later in this chapter—equanimity.

SYMPATHETIC JOY

In chapter 3, you might recall that we introduced joyfulness as one of the core aspects of the Mindful Warrior's code. Joyfulness was discussed in the context of breaking habitual thinking and response patterns, and learning to respond to adverse circumstances with happiness, clarity, and confidence. We would now like to discuss a particular dimension of joyfulness known as "sympathetic joy." Sympathetic joy means taking delight in the happiness of others, as well as in our own happiness. This joy plays an integral part in the cultivation of authentic loving-kindness and compassion.

In this industrialized and materialistic society, there is sometimes a tendency for people to resent those who achieve their dreams. For example, if a person has a lot of money, there is often an underlying assumption that they have somehow cheated other people or have been unscrupulous. The Mindful Warrior isn't interested in judging people or in pulling people down. Rather, they generate unselfish joy for the progress, success and happiness of others. If compassion is about identifying with the suffering of others, then sympathetic joy is about identifying with the successes and positive qualities of others.

When we manage to cultivate sympathetic joy effectively, it affects us and the people around us in a profound manner. People can become trapped in very negative thinking and behavioral patterns, but it is fascinating to watch them change as we practice sympathetic joy in their presence. Authentic sympathetic joy is infectious and it can be entertaining to observe how people change and begin to blossom in the presence of a Mindful Warrior who has managed to master this practice. A somber and miserable atmosphere can be quickly transformed into an atmosphere of happiness, vibrancy, and harmony. The Mindful Warrior sips from the spring of inner joy knowing that it is eternally available for them and everybody they encounter.

The Enemies of Sympathetic Joy

The close enemy of sympathetic joy is forced liveliness. This is similar to excitement, but it is a bit less spontaneous. Forced liveliness basically means acting with a level of energy and excitement that makes people feel uncomfortable. It's good to be enthusiastic, but there's a time and a place for this type of energy. If a person is intent on letting everybody know that they are happy and energetic, it invariably comes across as unnatural. A lot of public speakers do this—they overcompensate for nerves (and insecurity more generally) by injecting their talk with too much energy. Authentic sympathetic joy doesn't involve exhibitionism; it is spontaneous and unselfish.

The distant enemy of sympathetic joy is resentment. Theodore Dalrymple once said that resentment is one of the most futile and destructive of human emotions, and that people spend more time dwelling on the wrongs supposedly done to them than on the wrongs they have done to others. There is no room for resentment on the path of the Mindful Warrior.

Cultivating Sympathetic Joy

The following is a contemplation, or rather a series of contemplations, that can be used in order to cultivate sympathetic joy. These contemplations should ideally be practiced when you are in a comfortable and quiet environment. As you become more acquainted with this practice, it will become less important to start at the beginning and you might choose to focus on just one or two of the individual exercises.

1. Begin by reflecting on your own life situation in a positive manner and consider just how fortunate you are. You have eyes to see the world, ears to hear the world, a nose to smell the wonderful scents of the world, and a tongue to taste the flavors of the world. All of the abovementioned factors are a genuine cause for happiness. There are some people who do not have all of their sense faculties intact, and so if your sense faculties are still in working order, you are in a very privileged and fortunate position. You should breathe in and out in awareness and feel happy and content about your good fortune. If it happens to be the case that one or more of your sense faculties are not in good working order, you should still breathe in and out and feel genuinely content because, among many other things, you still have your breath. You are alive.

2. The next step in this contemplative exercise is to reflect upon additional aspects of your life that are a cause for joy. Per-

haps you have a job that provides you with a means to put food on the table and maintain a roof over your head. Perhaps you have free time to pursue your hobbies and interests, or to read books to relax or further your personal and spiritual development. Maybe you have a healthy and close relationship with your parents, partner, children, or friends. All of these are examples of things that we should feel joyful about.

While contemplating the various aspects of your life that are a cause for happiness, it is important to be sincere. The gratitude and joy that you generate must stem from a true intention. How many times have you said "thank you" to somebody without really meaning it? Therefore, when you practice being thankful and joyful for the pleasing things in your life, try to be enthusiastic and sincere—allow a sensation of joy to well up in your abdomen.

3. The next step in the process of cultivating sympathetic joy is to focus on more generic factors that are a cause of happiness, and at the same time allow the sensation of joy mentioned above to start to grow in intensity. By generic factors we mean taking joy in such things as the shining sun, or the rain that is falling and nourishing the plants and trees. Without the sun or rain, we would all be dead. The same applies to the trees that breathe out oxygen, bees that pollinate the plants, and insects that help to break down organic matter. All of these things are miracles that help to keep us alive.

The Mindful Warrior doesn't take things for granted and they know that their life is dependent on all other phenomena. Due to this understanding, they are able to be joyful about what other people might deem to be mundane or everyday occurrences. This is because the Mindful Warrior knows that there is no such thing as an everyday occurrence. Everything that happens occurs for the first and last time. There is also no such thing as "mundane" because everything in the universe, including the spider that has crawled into the bathroom sink, is entirely unique.

4. As the feeling of joy continues to well up inside you, begin to bathe in it and allow yourself to feel truly alive. When you feel ready to do so, the next step is to reflect upon the positive qual-

ities, happiness, and success of others. There could be a colleague at work who is happy because they have just been promoted. Or maybe somebody you know has recently commenced a loving relationship. Breathe in and out and generate feelings of great joy and happiness for these people. Of course, all things are impermanent and although these people are experiencing success and happiness in this moment, it won't last forever. Therefore, together with feelings of joy, you should generate compassion for these people because this happiness is only temporary. Perhaps this is why joy in the context of the Four Sublime Attitudes (the *brahmaviharahs*) that we referred to earlier is called "sympathetic joy."

This particular stage of the contemplative exercise should not be confused with the generation of pride. For example, perhaps you are a mother or father and you naturally feel proud because your children are doing well in school. However, this type of feeling is not what we mean when we talk about taking joy in other people's happiness and success. Sympathetic joy is more generous and open than pride (which is arguably more closed and self-oriented).

5. The next stage of the contemplative exercise requires a greater degree of abstract thinking. It involves reflecting on the difficulties that you are currently experiencing in your lives, and taking joy from them. These could be relationship difficulties with family members, partners, or friends. Alternatively, it could be a situation at work that you are feeling particularly resentful about. Other examples would be a traumatic event that you experienced in the past, or an ongoing situation that makes you feel anxious or stressed.

If you are experiencing suffering in this moment due to a painful or a distressing illness, then this is also a suitable subject to reflect upon for this part of the exercise. However, before you call to mind and reflect upon a particular difficulty that you are experiencing, please make sure that you are rooted in the present moment, and are feeling calm and stable. After having cultivated a centered and joyful mind, you can then select and focus on just one particular difficult aspect of your life. Begin by examining it from the point of view of a neutral onlooker. Remaining an on-looker will help to objectify the situation and this, in turn, should help you to examine the situation clearly and without the biasing effects of negative emotions.

Let's imagine, for the purposes of helping to explain this part of the contemplation, that the situation that is causing you distress relates to the words or actions of a person who is dear to you. Perhaps the person in question has been unskillful and has hurt you. Maybe they did not act responsibly with the love and trust that you placed in them. However, rather than dwell on their actions per se, consider the notion that, in conjunction with other difficult situations you have endured, the distress that this person has caused you influenced your decision to search for a way to overcome your suffering. In other words, if people didn't tangibly experience suffering, then they wouldn't be motivated to search for a path that leads to the end of suffering. By examining the situation objectively and with clarity, you can regard the person who caused you to suffer as your greatest teacher. They have given you a tremendous gift—an opportunity to grow in wisdom, aware-ness, and compassion. This is something to be joyful about.

By investigating your feelings, you should also be able to accept that, at least to a certain extent, the suffering that you endured (or are currently enduring) is heavily influenced by your own inter-pretation of events. Perhaps you built up expectations and ideas about how you would like your relationship with the person to unfold, and when these expectations were not met, it caused you to suffer. When we have lots of expectations, it means that we are trying to predict the future. If we try to predict the future, it means that we are not living in the here and now, and are not experiencing life on a moment-by-moment basis. Living in the future means that we are not experiencing the present moment for what it is.

By understanding that we are the biggest contributor to our own suffering, it helps to change the way we look at the difficulties we experience in life. If we didn't build up expectations and always make things about the me, the mine, and the I, we would suffer less. If we dwell on and become consumed by the pain another person has caused us, it isn't going to help us in any way. That person did what they did. They are who they are. We shouldn't try to make them into a saint or somebody that they are not. They will have their own perspective on the situation and it will likely differ from our own. In fact, there is a strong chance that their actions were a response to suffering that we or somebody else knowingly or unknowingly caused them.

By changing our relationship to the situation that has caused (or is causing) us to suffer, we learn to transform suffering and use it as a cause for cultivating happiness. Without suffering, it would be impossible to cultivate tranquility and joy. For this reason, the Mindful Warrior is comfortable with their suffering. They accept it and don't try to run from it. They understand that suffering is the only reason the path of the Mindful Warrior exists.

Thus, for this crucial part of the contemplation, breathe in and look deeply at your suffering, then breathe out and smile gently and knowingly toward yourself. Breathe in and observe situations that have caused you to suffer, then breathe out and let go of these situations. Breathe in and cultivate joy because you understand and accept suffering, then breathe out and allow this joy to per-meate every cell of your body. Breathe in and cultivate joy at the center of your heart, then breathe out and share this joy with the people and situations that have caused you to suffer.

6. This contemplative exercise in cultivating sympathetic joy concludes with simply returning awareness to the natural flow of the in-breath and out-breath, and making sure that tension has not been introduced into the body or mind (i.e., due to reflecting upon suffering as described above). Begin by mentally scanning the body to see if it is relaxed and settled. Then consciously place tension into your toes as you breathe in, and relax that tension as you breathe out. Do the same with your lower legs, upper legs, pelvis area, and stomach—place tension with the in-breath, and release the tension with the out-breath. Start with the lower parts of the body and continue to work your way upward. Take a little

more time when you arrive at the shoulders and neck, making sure that you allow them to completely relax.

EQUANIMITY

The Pāli term *upekkha* is rendered in English as "equanimity." This English word comes from the Latin *aequanimitas*, which means having an even mind, a psychological state of steadiness and calm. Equanimity is one of the foundation stones of meditation, and it facilitates the cultivation of spiritual peace as well as confidence in one's own being. The changing winds of life mean that we continuously encounter loss and gain, good-repute and ill-repute, praise and censure, as well as sorrow and happiness. However, while most people are driven by their emotions and thus blown here and there by life's changing circumstances, the Mindful Warrior remains absolutely steadfast. They remain a stable source of love and compassion for the suffering beings who are still stuck in soap opera living.

Often when people meet a Mindful Warrior who embodies and emanates authentic equanimity, they misinterpret the Mindful Warrior's stability and equipoise for indifference. However, indifference means not caring, whereas equanimity is all about remaining calm and centered so that one can care in an effective manner. Therefore, equanimity complements and completes the practices of loving-kindness, compassion, and sympathetic joy. Without a stable and even mind, the Mindful Warrior would likely be consumed by other people's suffering. Equanimity might therefore be thought of as the guardian that watches over loving-kindness and compassion, ensuring that they function in an optimum manner (i.e., without any of the close or distant enemies referred to above).

A key skill set that must be present to cultivate equanimity effectively is ethical awareness. Having a good intention and always acting in an ethically wholesome manner leads to a strong and undistracted mind. If we say and do things that are born from selfishness, it is very hard for equanimity to grow and flourish in the mind. Selfishness keeps us continuously embroiled in petty disputes and unskillful actions. However, when we practice ethical integrity, it is easy to give rise to stillness of mind as well as confidence in who we are and what we have done. If our thoughts, words, and actions stem from a right intention, then it doesn't matter how others choose to judge us. We can look at ourselves in the mirror and be completely content with who we are.

Equanimity is crucial if we wish to foster any kind of genuine spiritual insight. If we are centered and stable, we can see, hear, smell, taste, and touch things without conceptually adding to or subtracting from them. We can experience the present moment in all its splendor and beauty. Experiencing things just as they are is a prerequisite for understanding that there is essentially no difference between the mind and the objects that it perceives. However, if we perceive the objects and situations around us without equanimity, it is likely that we will develop strong emotions and attachments to those perceptions. These strong emotions will cause us to lose meditative awareness, and to fall back into soap opera living.

The Enemies of Equanimity

The close enemy of equanimity is indifference. If a person is indifferent, they do not care whether other people are happy or sad. People who are indifferent say things like *"it's not my problem," "who cares,"* and *"people have to deal with their own problems."* So long as their own needs and the needs of their immediate family or friends are met, the indifferent person isn't interested in what happens to other people.

Earlier in this chapter, we referred to compassion fatigue which can sometimes be a problem for people new to meditation. Indifference, on the other hand, is a problem that sometimes affects people who are (supposedly) further on in their meditation practice. They become indifferent because rather than use meditation to let go of themselves, they have practiced meditation in such a manner that they have become self-absorbed. They have become caught up in the idea that they are a 'meditator' who dwells in peace and who is spiritually superior to other people. They have turned their back on the Mindful Warrior principles, and on the world more generally.

The distant enemy of equanimity is attachment to people, objects, and situations. Because most people always want to be somewhere else or be somebody else, they are easily attracted to objects or situations that they deem will lead to something better. Due to attachment, the slightest sensory trigger (i.e., a sight, sound, smell, etc.) can cause a person to lose their clarity of perspective and find themselves saying and doing things that stem from unchecked emotion rather than from wisdom.

Cultivating Equanimity

There are several meditative techniques that can be used for cultivating equanimity. However, really and truly, equanimity is something that develops naturally when applying the Mindful Warrior principles during our day-to-day interactions. In other words, as we go through life and are exposed to certain adverse conditions, each time we respond with compassion, patience, joyfulness and wisdom, confidence in our own ability increases and we grow in equanimity.

Equanimity also arises from the understanding that while certain people and situations can be changed, others can't be. The essence of this wisdom is captured by the serenity prayer shown below. The serenity prayer is a lovely contemplation written by the American theologian Reinhold Niebuhr. If we can take to heart the meaning of the serenity prayer, then this will certainly facilitate the cultivation of equanimity:

> *God grant me the serenity to accept the things I cannot change*
> *The courage to change the things I can*
> *And the wisdom to know the difference.*

8

LETTING GO

Buddhist monks follow a code of conduct called the Vinaya code. Although Buddhist monastic traditions interpret the Vinaya code in different ways, some Buddhist monks—especially the less experienced ones—follow this code with great rigor and can be quite intransigent when it comes to deviating from the rules. One of the rules in the Vinaya code relates to comportment toward the opposite sex and states that: "Should any *bhikkhu* [monk], overcome by lust, with altered mind, engage in bodily contact with a woman, or in holding her hand, holding a lock of her hair or caressing any of her limbs, it entails initial and subsequent meetings of the community."

This is a fairly straightforward rule that is intended to prevent Buddhist monks—especially those that require and respond well to external discipline—from allowing desire and attachment to overpower the mind. However, it has unfortunately been taken to extremes by certain Buddhist monastic traditions where it is forbidden for a monk to touch a woman or even receive something from a woman directly. For example, in such Buddhist traditions, if a woman wishes to donate something to a monk (known as a *dana* offering), it must not be handed to the monk directly but must be placed on a cloth on the floor from where the monk may then pick it up.

In this chapter we discuss a very important practice that the Mindful Warrior has to master—the practice of "letting go." Training to be a Mindful Warrior is probably the hardest work that we will ever do. One of the reasons it is so challenging is because we have to "let go" of everything we think we know, including who we think we are. Letting go might sound like an easy thing to do, but it is not so easy in practice. There are many layers to the self that we have created and so while letting go might seem like a romantic undertaking, when the ego starts to feel threatened it can be tenacious in its efforts to assert itself. Before we discuss further the process and practice of letting go, we would like to recount one of our favorite stories about the dangers of holding on.

Two monks were making their way from one monastery to another. They had been practicing meditation together for many years and were very good friends. In fact, not only were they close friends, but there was also a teacher-student relationship in place—one of the monks was much older and had been a monk since long before the other monk was born. The journey was a long one and involved many days traveling on foot. As the two monks walked through the forests and countryside, they spent a great deal of time discussing various aspects of the Buddhist teachings.

At a certain point in their journey, the monks heard the screams of a woman coming from a nearby river. They hastily went to see what was happening and in the middle of the river, they saw a naked woman who was drowning. The older monk swiftly threw off his robes, dived into the water, and rescued the woman. He brought the naked woman to the banks of the river and proceeded to cover her with his spare robes. After assuring himself that she was safe and well, the two monks continued with the next leg of their journey.

However, the second part of their journey was quite different from the first. The river incident had quite an influence on the younger monk who, for the rest of the journey, had a surly comportment and refused to speak to the older monk. A few days later, the monks arrived at their destination—a monastery they were going to be staying at for the next few months. At this point, the young monk started to ostracize the older monk and refused to acknowledge his presence. The older monk was dismayed and began to worry about the comportment of his younger friend. One day the older monk decided to confront the younger monk by gently saying to him: "Please, young sir, why have you changed? What have I done to warrant being treated in this manner? If I have said or done something that has hurt you then I am truly sorry. I must have done it mindlessly and without intention."

The young monk replied: "You are not a true monk. You have broken the rules of the Vinaya Pitaka, and as such, I may no longer be associated with you." The older monk was rather shocked to hear this and asked what rules had been broken. The younger monk replied: "Not only did you touch a woman but you touched a naked woman and gave her the robes of a monk." The elder monk responded by saying: "How very true, I saved the woman and carried her to the banks of the river. I made sure that she was warm and well and then I left her on the riverbank. However, it would appear that you are still carrying her with you."

A BOOK OF RULES

When we allow rules to govern our lives and hold us back in our spiritual progress, then we really have to ask ourselves whether we are allowing ignorance to rule our lives. Most people create (sometimes without knowing it) their own set of rules. They develop fixed ideas about what is right and wrong, what constitutes acceptable and unacceptable behavior, and which type of people are worthy of their friendship. In this manner, they start to build walls that close off the mind to new people and experiences. In short, people allow their mind to construct a prison around itself, and as they grow older, the prison becomes smaller and smaller.

We are not saying that rules aren't important. Indeed, in order for society to function effectively, there need to be rules that we all abide by. We need rules in order to live well and to help us interact with others in a healthy and adaptive manner. For example, if the neighbor's dog barks all night, we can't just get out of bed, pick up a gun and shoot it! The written and unwritten rules of society dictate that we should wait until an appropriate opportunity presents itself and, in a civilized manner, talk to the neighbor in order to resolve the matter.

However, in addition to adhering (or in some cases not adhering) to the laws of the land, people tend to make up and follow their own rules. As part of belonging to a particular group or tier of society, the rules that we make up dictate that we do not associate or have dealings with certain other groups, or with certain types of people. Consequently, invisible (or sometimes visible) barriers are constructed and people avoid having meaningful contact with those that do not fit the required criteria.

We are labeled by others and we label ourselves and others. We put tags on people such as "He's a rather nice chap," "She's a delightful person, just a little too quick to judge," and "That person is bad." We also consciously and subconsciously label their conduct and lifestyle as "appropriate," "inappropriate," "successful," or "unsuccessful." Through this continuous process of labeling and making up rules, our mind creates an image of a "me," a "mine," and an "I." We use other people and their behaviors as a reference point, and this helps us to construct our self-identity. We create a self that we believe is independent, autonomous, and separate from all other phenomena in the world. We also create a picture of what and where we think our place is in the world, and our mind clings on to these creations with a grim determination.

Let's take the example of the young violent offender. There are certain rules that they are expected to abide by if they are to retain their position in their particular peer group, and in society more generally. More often than not, the rules of the violent offender's world mean that their mind ends up being full of anger, violence, and hatred (including toward themselves). If they end up spending time in prison, there is a strong chance that the cycle of violence and negativity that they have entered into will intensify.

Responding with fear and anger can become their normal mode of being, and it is easy for such people to feel that there is no way out. This feeling of being trapped often makes the young offender cling even tighter to their self-identity, and to the rules that define the world they live in. Consequently, for the young person involved in crime to stop abiding by the destructive rules of their inner and outer world, it often takes somebody external to that world to come along and help them understand that if they have the power to create such an identity, then they also have the power to dismantle it.

The path of the Mindful Warrior is concerned with dismantling and rewriting the self-created rules that underlie all of our thoughts, words, and actions. It doesn't matter if we abide by the rules of a criminal or pillar of society, a materialist or an idealist, a young person or an old person, a man or a woman, or a capitalist as opposed to a socialist, we have to learn to let go of who we think we are. If we are courageous and humble enough to at least entertain the idea that we have fallen into the trap of viewing ourselves and the world through a dense medium of self-imposed rules, labels, and fixed ideas, then we maximize our chances of being receptive to, and successfully assimilating, the principles of mindful warriorship.

LIGHTENING THE LOAD

When we are born, our minds are empty or free, so to speak. We see an object and we pick it up. Perhaps we shake it to see if it makes a sound. We smell it, look at it, and invariably we put it into our mouths in order to taste it. In short, we explore it because it is a new experience. Then we see another object worth exploring, and once again we engage in this process of investigation. After a while, we may return to the first object and because our minds are not cluttered up with thoughts, feelings, and mental chatter, we see the first object as though for the first time. We see and explore it as a fresh experience. However, at some point during the process of growing into an adult, things begin to change.

Imagine that the thoughts, feelings, and mental formations moving through the mind are like pieces of straw. During our infant years, the pieces of straw can be easily managed because they arise in the mind just a few at a time. At this stage in our development, we are able to make neat bundles or bales of straw and, for a short time, everything is fairly orderly and organized. However, as we grow older, the quantity of objects moving through the mind increases exponentially, and they start to bombard us at ever-increasing speed. We try to organize and make sense of as many of them as possible but there comes a point where we no longer have the discipline or ability to arrange all of the pieces of straw into neat bales. We eventually end up racing through life weighted down by an enormous and disorganized pile of straw that we carry around on our shoulders. It gets so big that it covers our head, eyes, ears, and nose. Consequently, everything we see, hear, smell, taste, and touch is filtered through, and therefore colored by, a disordered mound of thoughts, feelings, and mental formations.

Do you remember the three choices we outlined in chapter 2? They were:

1. *Allow your mind (with all of its emotions and mental chatter) to live your life for you;*
2. *Allow the minds of others (likewise full of emotions and mental chatter) to live your life for you;* or
3. *Live your life without the interference of either your own or another persons' unruly mind.*

If we live our lives according to the ethos of the first or second choice, this is basically the same as the person described above who ends up living each day under the weight and handicap of a heavy and disorganized pile of straw. However, if we live our lives according to the ethos of the third choice, then to a certain extent, we become like a baby or infant again. We maximize our chances of being able to see all experiences as new and miraculous, and this way of perceiving the world makes it easy to organize the straw into orderly bales. In fact, by learning to dwell in the present moment and see it as fresh and unique, we eventually learn not to hold onto the pieces of straw in the first place. We learn to let go of feelings, thoughts, and concepts as they arise in the mind. Consequently, we move beyond the stage of having to "organize" the contents of the mind, and we cultivate a mind that is light, free, and completely unburdened.

People sometimes ask how it is possible to be free of concepts while engaging in everyday work and life activities. In other words, to function in the world, we need to think, plan, and form ideas. However, it's not the case that the Mindful Warrior does not give rise to thoughts, ideas, or concepts, it's just that they don't hold on to them. The Mindful Warrior understands that when we plan, for all intents and purposes, we create a container or mold that we believe, or hope, the future will fit into. But from the moment we formulate a plan, the conditions around us start to change. This means that no matter how much we wish the container to function correctly, it often ends up being the wrong shape. It is not the act of making a container that causes us problems, but difficulties arise when we become attached to the container, and try to force our situation to fit it. Furthermore, people often make plans with a limited or even biased perspective of what is happening inside and around them. This means that even from the very beginning, their container was probably the wrong shape.

The Mindful Warrior plans as much as they need to, but they keep some "breathing space" around their plans. They understand that they are forming plans about the future, which is impossible to predict with 100 percent accuracy. Consequently, the Mindful Warrior's plans, concepts, and ideas are fluid constructions that they can adapt or let go of as required.

Among certain health care disciplines, there has been growing interest in the last decade in an illness known as fibromyalgia syndrome. The main symptoms of fibromyalgia are widespread bodily pain, poor quality of sleep, fatigue, and difficulty in remembering. The illness is also associated with poor quality of life, feeling anxious and depressed, and mobility impairments. Approximately 3 percent of adults are estimated to suffer from fibromyalgia, with higher rates in females compared to males. Very little is known about what causes fibromyalgia, and the illness is proving to be difficult to treat. It is our opinion that not knowing how to handle and let go of mental clutter (i.e., being weighed down by a heavy and disorganized bundle of straw) plays an important role in the onset of illnesses such as fibromyalgia. In fact, fibromyalgia might be one example of how psychological distress can spill over onto the body in the form of pain and fatigue. Based on our own research, individuals with fibromyalgia generally respond well to mindfulness because it helps them to let go of emotional baggage, and to rewrite the rules that they have chosen to live by.

DECONSTRUCTING THE SELF

Although we are the principal creator of our "self," in general, the process of creation is not something that we have engaged in consciously. It is something that has tended to just happen. In other words, during the process of simply engaging in and getting on with our life, we suddenly ended up having a very firm sense of a me, mine, and I. It is as though we have inadvertently built (and allowed others to build) a great mansion with many rooms in it. Each room reflects a different part of who we are. Maybe we are one person when we are with our spouse and family, but are a different person when we are at work. We might be one person with one friend, but a totally different person with another friend. Maybe we are one person when we are at home, but a different person when on holiday. Likewise, perhaps we are a different person when things are going well compared to when things are not going favorably for us.

Consider taking a few moments in order to explore just how many different types of "I" you have created. There is absolutely nothing wrong with the fact that we have many different "I's." We perform many different roles, and so to a certain degree, it is inevitable that we comport and present ourselves in different ways. Please try to be honest with yourself when reflecting in this manner. How many different rooms are there in your mansion? Some of the things that you find in the various rooms might not be pleasant, but don't worry about it. They are just rooms that contain things—they remain something that you observe. If you like, you can step inside one of these rooms and sit there for a while, but try not to touch anything for now.

While walking through the mansion of the mind, you will probably find that you have used a substantial amount of construction material. However, although each room is brimming with content, most of it is likely to be of limited value. When you start to realize this, try to avoid the urge to do some spring cleaning. Instead of cleaning the mansion, what we are going to do is to actually pull it down altogether, dismantling all the rules we have learned to live by.

During the process of deconstructing the mansion, an important consideration to bear in mind is that because each of our thoughts, words, and actions have made us who and what we are today, we cannot simply erase that which has taken place. Therefore, as we dismantle the mansion of the self, it will be necessary to carry out some recycling. As we deconstruct the mansion of self, we should separate the deconstructed material into two different mounds. One mound is for material that can be recycled and used in the new build. The other mound is for material that we wish to discard altogether.

Once we have taken the mansion down brick by brick, label by label, rule by rule, and concept by concept, we clear the ground in preparation for installing new foundations. It is hopeless and unproductive to try to rebuild on ground that is unstable and full of rubbish. Sweeping the ground completely clear gives us the best chance of building something stable and strong.

Amid this cleared ground that is bordered by a small mound of recyclable material, we take a moment just to sit in that clear space for a while. We sit in the clear and empty ground space of the mind. In this space there are absolutely no rules that we have to abide by. There are no me, mine, or I entities that we have to be. We have let go of them all. There is nobody that we need to impress—not even ourselves. Here in this empty ground space of the mind, there is just simply being.

After having taken some time to recognize and enjoy the empty ground of the mind, we can begin the process of reconstruction. However, the new "self" that we are going to create will be quite different from the old one. In fact, although we are going to construct a new "self," it won't be a self that can be pinpointed to a specific location in time and space. It will be a dynamic entity that works in harmony with the changing conditions around it. Much like a shimmering mirage, the new self won't be something that can defined using labels, rules or concepts.

The way that this new "self" relates to life is actually very similar to the experience of dwelling in the clear and empty ground of the mind that we referred to above. The only difference is that in order to effectively interact with those with whom we share this world, there needs to be a "self" that others can relate to. However, really and truly, this self is just a manifestation of the empty ground of the mind. The clear and empty ground space of the mind manifests as a "self" and plays its part in the world, but it has let go of any attachment to the idea of being a self. This "selfless self" is dynamic, adaptive, and free. It is the self of an authentic Mindful Warrior.

SITTING AT THE CENTER OF THE UNIVERSE

The following is an exercise to help establish and orient ourselves in the empty ground of the mind, and to rebuild a dynamic and selfless self. Imagine that you are sitting at the center of the universe—not as a body or form but simply as naked energy. Breathe and relax. Observe the suns, moons, and planets all around you. Observe them coming into being, observe them living, and observe them passing away. Things become and things dissolve.

Breathe in and see that the universe breathes in with you. Breathe out and see that the universe breathes out with you. You and the universe are simply energy that becomes and dissolves.

1. ***Solid as a mountain:*** As you breathe in, collect together the naked energy and allow it to gently transform into a mountain. See yourself as a mountain with roots deep in the earth and summit high in the sky. As you breathe in with calm, observe the winds of the mind as they blow against the mountain. The mind blows thoughts, feelings, and mental chatter. Sometimes the sun shines, sometimes the rain falls, and sometimes the mountain is set upon by an angry blizzard. However, you sit and breathe knowing that you are not those thoughts or feelings, and they are not you. As you breathe out you realize and feel that you are solid and completely stable. Enjoy being here for a few moments.

   When you feel ready to do so, let go of the mountain and allow it to dissolve back into the earth. Remember that all things change. The mountain dissolves into the earth, and the earth, in turn, dissolves into the universe. Finally, allow the universe to dissolve into you so that once again, you become simply energy. From here observe that things become and things dissolve. Breathe, relax, and let go.

2. ***Fresh as a flower:*** As you breathe in, collect together the naked energy and allow it to gently transform into a flower. See yourself as a flower with roots deep in the earth. As you breathe in with calm, observe the winds of the mind as they blow thoughts, feelings, and mental chatter. Breathe and relax, allow the flower to bend as the winds of the mind blow over it. When the winds have died down, the flower once again stands erect and beautiful. Dewdrops form on the petals of the flower, and it bathes in the morning rays of the sun. Allow yourself to feel refreshed by the dewdrops. Enjoy being here for a few moments.

   When you feel ready to do so, let go of the flower and remember that all things change. Do as you did with the

mountain and allow the flower to dissolve back into the
earth. Then allow the earth, in turn, to dissolve into the
universe. Finally, allow the universe to dissolve into you so
that once again, you become simply energy. From here observe that things become and things dissolve. Breathe, relax
and let go.

3. ***Free as a cloud in the sky***: As you breathe in, collect
together the naked energy and allow it to gently transform
into a cloud. See yourself as a cloud that is light, white, and
free in the sky. As you breathe in with calm, observe the
winds of the mind as they blow through the cloud. See how
those winds of thoughts, feelings, and mental chatter are
leaving behind particles of themselves. Subtly, we are clinging on, even if we don't really want to. As those winds continue to blow, the cloud accumulates those particles and it
becomes heavier and darker, until it is black and ominous.
But we sit and breathe. We understand that all things
change. We are not the contents of the cloud and they are
not us. Enjoy being here for a few moments.

When you feel ready, let go of all those accumulated particles, and allow them to fall as rain and dissolve back into the
earth. As you let go, the cloud once again becomes light,
white, and totally free in the sky. Once the rain has dissolved
into the earth, allow the earth, in turn, to dissolve into the
universe. Finally, allow the universe to dissolve into you so
that once again, you become simply energy. From here,
observe that things become and things dissolve. Breathe,
relax, and let go.

4. ***Calm as still water that reflects:*** As you breathe in, collect together the naked energy and allow it to gently transform into a lake. See yourself as a lake of calm, still water
and observe those mind winds as they cause the surface of
the lake to ripple. Sit and breathe with patience and understanding, and allow the winds to pass you by. In time, the
lake becomes totally calm again, and it reflects all that is. It
reflects the mountain that is solid, the flower that is fresh,

and the cloud that is free in the sky. The lake also reflects each and every drop of rain that falls from the cloud. While dwelling as calm still water, allow the realization to arise that all of those raindrops—your thoughts, feelings, and mental chatter—are simply reflections without substance. Enjoy being here for a few moments.

When you feel ready to do so, let go of the lake and remember that all things change. Allow the lake to dissolve back into the earth. Then allow the earth, in turn, to dissolve into the universe. Finally, allow the universe to dissolve into you so that once again, you become simply energy. From here observe that things become and things dissolve. Breathe, relax, and let go.

5. *A precious human life* : As you breathe in, collect together the naked energy and allow it to gently transform into the extremely precious entity known as a human being. Attend to your breathing and observe the winds that blow through your mind. You have understood that the contents of the mind are not you, and that you are not them. Therefore, sit as solid as a mountain, fresh as a flower, free as a cloud in the sky, calm as still water that reflects, and instruct the mind to enjoy whatever is contained within this here and now, without adding to it or subtracting from it. Simply experience this precious moment exactly as it is. Then let it go in order to make space for the next precious moment. Enjoy being here for a few moments.

When you feel ready to do so, let go of this precious human body and remember that all things change. Allow the body to dissolve back into the earth. Then allow the earth, in turn, to dissolve into the universe. Finally, allow the universe to dissolve into you so that once again, you become simply energy. From here observe that things become and things dissolve. Breathe, relax, and let go.

Repeated practice of the meditation outlined above should facilitate the realization that all things are impermanent, including our thoughts, feelings, mental chatter, and so forth. As we will go on to discuss in the next chapter, since we know that all things are impermanent, it is illogical and futile for us to try to hold onto them in the first place. The selfless self of the Mindful Warrior delights in and dances with the present moment. Without rules, labels, and clutter, nothing can stick to their mind and weigh them down. An authentic Mindful Warrior is somebody who has completely let go of themselves, and who is not bound by the notion of a me, mine, or I.

9

MINDFULNESS OF BIRTH, MINDFULNESS OF DEATH

According to the US Central Intelligence Agency, approximately eight out of every one thousand people that were alive at the start of 2013 died during the following twelve months. This figure, known as the global mortality rate, means that almost 0.8 percent of the world's population dies every year. A figure of 0.8 percent may not sound like a lot, but based on the world's current population levels, it equates to 107 human deaths every minute—almost two deaths per second. If you are somebody that normally goes to bed at 10:30 p.m. and sleeps for eight hours, by the time you wake up each morning at 6:30 a.m., more than fifty thousand people have died. Death is incredibly common, far more common than most people would like to acknowledge. The most common cause of death is illness, including illness in old age. However, other reasonably common causes of death include accident, suicide, and homicide. Death can also be caused by completely random events, such as a lightning strike.

Despite the fact that death is a very common occurrence, people can be complacent about death and often fall into the trap of assuming it is something that will never happen to them. Being complacent about death can act as a major obstacle to progressing along the path of the Mindful Warrior. Impermanence and death are things that we encounter during every single moment of our lives, and if we choose not to see or be aware of these truths, then in addition to succumbing to cowardice, we are basically deceiving ourselves. The Mindful Warrior principles require us to be courageous enough to embrace death and to encompass impermanence into our field of awareness. If we fail to do this, if we don't put aside the time to cultivate a deep understanding of death and appreciate just how delicate life is, the likelihood is that we will leave this world full of fear, anguish, and regret.

LIFE: A NEAR DEATH EXPERIENCE

In the 1960s and 1970s, psychiatrist Elizabeth Kubler-Ross and psychologist and medic Raymond Moody played a pivotal role in bringing the phenomenon of near-death experience (NDE) to the attention of both the general public and the wider scientific community. The scientific study of NDEs—especially prior to the 1990s—met with a certain amount of skepticism among psychologists and medical professionals. However, in recent years, the psychological and medical community have become increasingly open to the possibility that the NDE is a bona fide phenomenon that falls within the range of human experience. The NDE is typically associated with a particular set or pattern of experiences that may occur when a person is close to dying, when they believe they are close to dying, or when they find themselves in the period between clinical death and resuscitation. NDEs often involve one, or a combination of, the following features: (i) an out of body experience, (ii) the experience of moving through a tunnel, (iii) communicating with a being of light, (iv) meeting with deceased persons, and/or (v) a life review. Based on these characteristics or "diagnostic" criteria, NDEs are not particularly common occurrences. However, by slightly altering the defining criteria, we would actually argue that every single sentient being is currently partaking in a "near death experience."

From the moment we are born, each second that passes brings us closer to our death. Even being young does not provide any assurance of life, as death can strike at any age. Indeed, some people die while still in the womb, some in infancy, and some in adolescence. Some people die in the prime of adulthood and some in old age. Life is like the sand moving through an hour-glass— some people start with more sand than others, but sooner or later it runs out just the same. We are born, we live, and we will die.

The human body is a beautiful and wondrous entity but invincibility is not one of its strengths. A small prick by a sharp object, contact with a hot pan, a finger trapped in a door—these are just a few examples of how the smallest mishap can cause tremendous discomfort and pain. In fact, there only has to be the slightest imbalance in the external environment and the human body starts to rapidly shut down. Environmental conditions such as being too hot, being too cold, a shortage of water, or a lack of food can all quickly lead to death. Even such minor things as eating a mouthful of spoiled food, catching a common flu bug, or slipping on ice can lead to death. In fact, at any one time, the only thing that separates us from death is a single breath in or out. It is as though the human being operates a "just in time" survival system which means that the slightest delay in taking in air, water, food, or medicine can be fatal. This is what the Buddha is reported to have said about the fleeting nature of life:

> This existence of ours is as transient as autumn leaves. To watch the birth and death of beings is like looking at the movements of a dance. A lifetime is like a flash of lightning in the sky, rushing by, like a torrent down a steep mountain.

THE LIFE GAMBLE

In terms of cultivating a profound awareness of death, and of earnestly applying ourselves to spiritual practice, it seems that some people are reluctant to do so because they believe that death represents the end of their existence. This relates to a dilemma that we call "the life gamble"—the simple choice of whether to engage in spiritual practice. This is a "primordial choice" that transcends religion, ethnicity, wealth, sex, and culture. In fact, since this is a choice that affects everybody equally, all human beings might be referred to as "life gamblers." On the one hand, the life gambler can choose to adopt a self-centered outlook and bet "all-in" on the belief of no afterlife and no accountability for their actions in this life or beyond. After all, if this life is all there is, why should we waste our time thinking about anything other than mindlessly indulging ourselves? On the other hand, the life gambler can choose to "hedge their bets" by cultivating unconditional wellbeing during this life, and preparing themselves for death.

In terms of what happens during and after death, we would argue that the first scenario reflects a "high-risk low-reward" strategy, because if the life gambler is wrong and "mind-essence" continues beyond this lifetime, then there is a strong probability that they will experience anguish, regret, and disorientation when they die. The second scenario, therefore, reflects a "low-risk high-reward" strategy because if it transpires that there is no "existence" after death, then there will be no stream of consciousness to experience regret due to having needlessly engaged in spiritual practice. However, if it turns out that the thread of subtle-consciousness does indeed endure throughout successive lifetimes, then the life gambler not only reaps the benefit of spiritual practice during this life, but they are also better equipped to deal with whatever happens during and after death with greater confidence and awareness. Likewise, depending on whether one subscribes to the belief in reincarnation, the person who hedges their bets is also better positioned to further their spiritual progress during subsequent lifetimes until they attain liberation.

The saying "gambling with their life" is sometimes used to refer to people who engage in life-threatening or potentially harmful activities. However, if one accepts that reincarnation is at least a possibility, then the person who chooses not to earnestly engage in spiritual practice might be said to be "gambling with their life-times."

Whenever we are teaching Buddhist or non-Buddhist medita-tion practitioners, we always suggest that from time to time, they take a moment to consider which life-gambling strategy they are currently following. For example, if you are currently taking the high-risk low-reward approach and are mostly concerned with se-curing your own comfort and success during this life, then think about whether the short-term rewards outweigh the risk to your long-term spiritual wellbeing. Alternatively, if you consider your-self to be a spiritual practitioner (i.e., somebody taking a low-risk high-reward approach), then ask yourself whether your practice is on track or whether you are allowing your ego to fool or deceive you. For example, is your practice all about improving your public or professional image? Are you more interested in being seen to be mindful rather than truly internalizing the practice? Is your practice a means of spacing out to temporarily escape from your problems? Is your practice tangibly helping you to enter death with warrior-like fearlessness?

THE NATURAL LAW OF IMPERMANENCE

Whenever we are giving a talk on spiritual practice and state that nothing is permanent, there is invariably always somebody that doubts the truth of this natural law and tries to give an example of something that doesn't undergo change. However, the fact is that all phenomena, without exception, are subject to change and ulti-mately to dissolution. The human body is impermanent, friends and family are impermanent, the planet we live on is imperma-nent, and even the universe will ultimately cease to be. Absolutely nothing escapes the cycle of impermanence. Consider just how many powerful rulers and regimes there have been throughout history. Yet none of them have endured throughout time. Leaders are ousted, the oppressed become rulers, the rich become poor, and the poor become rich.

All phenomena are transient occurrences and are subject to ageing and decay. Because we can be certain that an object that currently exists will eventually cease to do so, we can safely assume that phenomena are not static but are continuously undergoing change. Therefore, there are two main aspects to the law of impermanence. The first is that all things die or dissolve, and the second is that phenomena are in a constant state of flux. Thus, although it might not seem to be the case, whenever we look at somebody or something, we are actually looking at impermanence in action. If we look at ourselves in the mirror and then do so again one hour later, it may seem that we have not changed. However, any scientist or doctor will tell you that this is not the case. Countless new cells in our body will have been produced and countless cells and compounds will have died or been broken down. In fact, not only will our body have changed, but our feelings and state of mind will have changed, the air and atmosphere around us will have changed, and, believe it or not, the mirror itself will also no longer be the same.

Impermanence is all around us. We breathe impermanence, we eat impermanence, and we drink impermanence. Impermanence is the basic fabric that comprises reality—if something exists, its fundamental nature is impermanence. However, although the law of impermanence means that everything is changing and ultimately has to die, it is because of impermanence that new things can be born. Indeed, without death, there could not be birth. If plants, insects, animals, and human beings did not die and decompose, there would be no food and energy available for future life to feed on.

Thus, impermanence is an essential building block of life. Death feeds birth and birth feeds death. Consequently, we should try not to look upon impermanence as a negative or sad thing. It is neither a good thing nor a bad thing. It is just something that is. The sooner we come to terms with impermanence and accept the fact that all things have to die, the easier it is for us to appreciate that making time to understand and prepare for death is something that we should not put off any longer. The Buddha explained this principle as follows:

> Do not pursue the past. Do not lose yourself in the future. The past is history. The future is yet to come. Looking deeply at life as it is in the here and now, the practitioner dwells, unshaken and free in heart. We must be diligent today, as death may strike tomorrow, for there is no bargaining with the lord of death. [1]

MAKING TIME FOR DEATH

In our experience, any complacency regarding death quickly disappears when people find themselves at death's door. Indeed, as Buddhist teachers who are sometimes requested to visit people that are dying, it is sadly frequent for us to see strong feelings of regret, anger, and fear among people who know they are on the cusp of death. You might think that when it is time to die it is easy to switch off and just let go of things. Unfortunately, though, it doesn't work like that. Indeed, it is often the case that at death, a person's attachment and clinging to family, friends, possessions, and reputation becomes even more fierce and overpowering. However, when the last few grains of sand are about to slip through the hour glass, money, belongings, family, and status count for nothing. They cannot be carried forward. We have to leave life in exactly the same manner that we entered it—alone and without possessions.

If you have spent a lot of time with people that are in their last moments of life, you may have observed a reasonably common scenario or pattern of behavior. It happens about midway into what certain Buddhist teachings refer to as the "dying *bardo*" (*bardo* is a Tibetan word that means "in-between state"). The dying *bardo* basically refers to the period running up to and immediately before death. During this dying period, there often comes a point when the dying person is still cognizant enough to be aware of what is happening, but realizes that the end of their life is only a few hours or days away. At this point, whatever color remains in their face seems to disappear. In conjunction with this relatively sudden loss of complexion, a certain look comes over the person's face and eyes. It's a look that signifies a moment of spiritual insight and broadening of perspective, but also a feeling of total helplessness.

This sudden and temporary opening-up of the mind happens because as the body weakens and begins to slowly shut down, the mind becomes freer and less restricted. At this time, it is easier for a person to witness their life almost as an observer and to see it in the wider scheme of things. With this "spiritual perspective" that dawns at certain stages during the dying process, it is considerably easier for the individual to see that all the effort and worry they put into getting ahead and becoming a somebody was, ultimately, a waste. Their efforts may have resulted in some short-term reward, but more often than not, this did not help them evolve as a human being. In fact, in their labors to obtain the things they wanted, it is probable that they acted selfishly and hurt people in the process. This is why we said earlier that it is not unusual for people who are dying to be full of remorse.

It is not only when dying that the abovementioned experience of seeing the bigger picture dawns, because it can also happen during life. Sometimes it just happens out of the blue for no apparent reason—a sudden flash of insight that completely changes a person's entire perspective on life. However, usually these moments of spiritual insight are triggered by a significant or traumatic life event such as being involved in a serious accident or losing a loved one. Everybody—including those people that purport to have no interest in spiritual practice—experiences this moment of clear seeing at some point in their lives. However, the majority of people unfortunately choose to ignore the significance of this moment or decide that they will focus on spiritual development when they are older and have more spare time.

Although it is never too late to turn to spiritual practice, death is something that tends to creep up on people without them expecting it. In the final stages, there is not a great deal that can be done to change the way a person sees themselves and their place in life. The human condition is truly amazing—as human beings, there really are no limits to how much we can develop and expand the mind. However, if we leave things until it is too late and choose not to embrace the Mindful Warrior principles, then we are like a person that endures all kinds of adversities in order to travel to an island of gold but who then forgets why they are there and leaves empty-handed.

MINDFULNESS OF DEATH

You might think that it is inappropriate or unfair of us to discuss the reality of death in as direct and open a manner as we are here. However, we believe that the sooner a person begins to fully accept that at some undefined point they will die, the sooner they can begin to prepare themselves for death rather than waiting until it is too late. In this manner, we are being completely honest and transparent with ourselves, and with the nature of reality more generally. As soon as we stop trying to hide from death or pretend that we are immune to it, we find that it becomes much easier to breathe, and we immediately feel more confident, relaxed, and at ease.

In terms of gradually developing an awareness of death, one effective way to do this is to conclude each meditation session with a few minutes specifically contemplating the impermanent nature of ourselves, and of phenomena more generally. Then it is a case of carrying this awareness forward such that we remember to be aware of impermanence as we go about our daily tasks. We definitely shouldn't be going around constantly repeating to ourselves that things are impermanent, but it does take a conscious effort in order to develop the clear vision that allows us to perceive impermanence at all times. A further technique for cultivating awareness of impermanence is to practice meditations that are specifically focused on dying and/or death. Such meditations invariably involve sitting in equanimity and mindfully visualizing one's corpse as it progresses through the process of decay and dissolution following death. For a detailed example of such a meditation, you could read the nine "charnel ground contemplations" that appear in key Buddhist teachings on mindfulness, including the *satipatthāna sutta*, *mahasatipatthāna sutta*, and *kāyagatāsati sutta*.

You will know when your mindfulness of death practice is hitting the mark because with every single breath and heartbeat, you become profoundly aware of the uncertainty of the time of death, as well as its inevitability. Formerly stressful situations will no longer faze you and your perspective on life will become vast and spacious. If a person comes to you with a gripe or complaint, rather than flaring up or responding with a clever remark, you will be able to take a step back and respond with compassion and gentleness. You will see just how foolish it is to fight or squabble, and without any deliberate effort on your part, you will feel genuine love and kindness for the person that is suffering in front of you.

Mindfulness of death helps us to prioritize what is important in life. If you are stressed because of your job, finances, health, or relationships, perhaps you should ask yourself whether there is really any value in getting worked up about these things. A hundred years from now, it is guaranteed that both you and the person or situation causing you worry will no longer exist. In fact, can you be certain that you will remain alive or healthy for even one more day? We are not saying that you should constantly worry about death, but appreciating fully that death is never too far away can help put things in perspective.

The beautiful thing is that by allowing the realization of impermanence to infuse our being, we can gradually learn not to hold onto things too tightly. This means that when the people and things that we love are present, we can truly cherish them, but when they dissolve, we can let go of them more freely. Indeed, research demonstrates that an increased acceptance and internalization of impermanence can actually buffer against psychological distress and assist with recovery and growth following exposure to traumatic situations. For example, the grief process is generally understood to begin with a period of shock and then move through phases of distress and denial, mourning, and eventually recovery. However, a greater familiarization with the impermanent nature of life is believed to exert a form of resilience effect that can soften the grieving process and bring about the earlier onset of the recovery phase. This is consistent with findings from our own research, which demonstrate that practicing mindfulness of impermanence can help people to let go of psychological pain, as well as be a joyful and spiritually enriching experience.

Every time we do something, we do it for the first and last time. Every breath is a new one. The present moment vanishes at exactly the same instant it manifests. The recognition of this can help us to invest the things we do and say with great meaning. All phenomena are transient; they cannot endure even if they want to. Therefore, let experience unfold without clinging to it. Thoroughly enjoy the practice of sitting in stillness and observing the birth and death of phenomena.

BEYOND DEATH

Initially, the practice of mindfulness of impermanence is concerned with deeply appreciating that life truly is precious and that death is a question of when rather than if. However, by simply observing the present moment and remaining calm and in stillness no matter what occurs, we are also actually preparing ourselves for moving through death with composure and fearlessness. Depending upon how far we advance along the Mindful Warrior's path, our understanding of what happens during death will change. Initially, death may be a complete mystery but as we continue to explore our inner self, it is possible that certain meditative experiences relating to death will transpire. We should try not to see such experiences as mystical or particularly special, because many dedicated spiritual practitioners report having encountered them at some point in their contemplative journey. However, even if we don't quite catch a glimpse of what it is like to be dead while we are still alive, whatever preparations we make by practicing mindfulness will certainly not be in vain.

In fact, even if we haven't yet embarked on an authentic spiritual path and therefore haven't made any preparations for death, there is no point in fearing death. Fear of death is basically fear of the unknown. However, for this very reason—that we don't know what is going to happen when we die—there is no point in being frightened. Just because we can't conceive of something, it doesn't mean we should be scared of it. This is a very important consideration because the mind is incredibly powerful, particularly during death. In fact, if we enter death with fear, then it is highly probable that the experience will be very frightening. Therefore, given that we don't know for sure what is going to transpire when we die, the most sensible thing to do is to enter death without fear and with an open, compassionate, and generous mind.

According to certain Buddhist texts, as the mind begins to withdraw from the body and subtler forms of consciousness become dominant, we experience various sensations, sounds, and visions. Examples include the smell and sight of smoke and fireflies, feeling very heavy and unable to move, feeling incredibly light, feeling hot, feeling cold, seeing bright lights and images, feeling that we cannot breathe or are surrounded by water, hearing loud sounds and thunder claps, encountering other beings (including both celestial and wrathful presences), traveling at the speed of thought, and moving through solid objects. However, much like a dream, these visions and death experiences are none other than the product of our own mind. Therefore, all we have to do is sit in equanimity and observe them. We know that they are impermanent and so we should let them come and go. If we become attached or have aversion toward these mental projections, then—according to the Buddhist teachings—there is a strong probability that we will fuel them and that they will overpower us.

Thus, just as when we are alive, what we experience during death is directly influenced by our own perception and by our ability to let go. If you stop and think about it, in the examples given above of the types of experiences that might be encountered during and after death, there isn't really anything that is tremendously different from the types of things we experience when we are alive or dreaming. We meet pleasant and unpleasant people all the time, we feel hot and cold, we hear sudden and loud noises, and we do strange things when dreaming including flying through the sky.

The truth is that at the ultimate or absolute level, birth, life, and death are manmade concepts. The word *birth* implies that something begins and the word *death* implies that something ends. However, according to Buddhist thought, this is not quite accurate because birth, life, and death are phases that continue to manifest from within a single continuum of mind. For example, when we go to sleep and start dreaming, it is as though one phase of our life comes to a temporary end (i.e., waking reality), and another phase begins (i.e., dreamt reality). We repeat this cycle every twenty-four hours. However, for any given dream to begin, there has to be a mind already in existence from which the dream consciousness can manifest. Likewise, when the dream finishes and we wake up, there must exist a mind from which the waking-state consciousness can manifest. The sky might be full of gray clouds one day, and white clouds another day. But the sky itself doesn't go anywhere; it just continues to serve as the medium within which different types of cloud can manifest.

Although it appears as though one phase of our life dies and another one begins each time we wake from a dream, all that is happening is that the mind is continuing with its ongoing cycle of giving rise to different types of consciousness. The exact same thing happens when we die—the mind gives rise to a particular type of consciousness, but the mind itself doesn't go anywhere. Thus, as we will explain further in the next chapter, when we die there actually isn't any coming or going. Ultimately, there is nothing to let go of, and nothing to hold on to.

We would like to finish this chapter on impermanence and mindfulness of death with a short reflection that we wrote called 'A Bubble in the Wind':

> *Life is like a bubble carried by the wind. Some bubbles burst sooner; others burst later. Some bubbles burst of their own accord; others burst by accident. Some bubbles are deliberately burst. However, one way or another, all bubbles burst. The Mindful Warrior recognizes they are not only the bubble, but are also the wind that gently carries it along. That wind has no point of origin and is without destination. It blows freely wherever it likes. How wonderful!*

10

THE EMPTY SELF

Throughout this book, we have made numerous direct and indirect references to the fact that human beings (and indeed all phenomena) are empty of an intrinsically existing self. "Non-self" and "emptiness" are perhaps two of the most poorly understood principles of meditation. Upon encountering the notion of emptiness, people either tend to become frightened and associate emptiness with complete nothingness, or they relate to emptiness purely on the level of the intellect. As far as the Mindful Warrior is concerned, emptiness is a place that they consider home, and they allow their realization of emptiness to infuse all of their thoughts, words, and actions. However, as part of their intimate relationship with emptiness, the Mindful Warrior is fully aware of the risks that exist when attempting to experientially assimilate emptiness into their being. In this chapter, we explore the notion of the "empty self" in more detail, and outline steps that can be taken to ensure that an individual's engagement with emptiness remains something that promotes, rather than hinders, spiritual growth.

When reading about emptiness in this chapter, please try to practice some of the basic mindfulness principles that were introduced earlier in the book. If we read about emptiness with a mind that is calm, present, and free of preconceived ideas, then there is a greater chance we will be able to use our intuition in order to grasp what emptiness is all about. However, if we approach topics such as emptiness purely on the academic level, then it is likely that we will miss the point. Don't worry if you initially don't fully understand some of the ideas explored in this chapter. If you continue with your day-to-day practice of meditative awareness, and then come back to this chapter at another point in time, you might find that the meaning becomes more apparent. Just like the bulb of a flower that needs to absorb the heat of the sun before it produces a shoot, sometimes understanding needs to bake in the light of awareness before it blossoms in the mind.

EMPTINESS AND FULLNESS

So far in this book, we have mostly discussed emptiness from the point of view of interconnectedness. Since phenomena do not exist as standalone entities, it means that they do not possess a self that exists independently of all other things. When we breathe in, a part of our in-breath contains some of other people's out-breath. In fact, it is possible that our in-breath comprises some breath particles that were once exhaled by individuals such as Shakyamuni Buddha or Jesus Christ. When we breathe out, we exhale what will become the in-breath of the trees and the living beings with whom we inhabit this earth. From this point of view, there is really only one breath that flows through everything. As beings are born, they connect to and share in this universal breath, and through the process of breathing, they sustain the life of others just as much as they sustain their own life.

In much the same way that there is a universal breath of life, there is also a universal river of life. When we drink water, we consume the clouds, rivers, oceans, and rain. Since the human body comprises approximately 60 percent water, this means that we are made of 60 percent rain and clouds. Likewise, when we urinate and perspire, we help to create clouds and rain, and to keep the rivers and oceans full. As beings are born, they connect to and share in the universal river of life, and through the processes of drinking, perspiring, and passing water, they sustain the life of others just as much as they sustain their own life. When we drink from the universal river of life, we also inhale part of the universal breath of life because water contains small particles of air. Likewise, when we breathe in air from the universal breath, we also drink from the universal river of life because air contains small particles of water. Therefore, the universal breath of life and the universal river of life are really one and the same thing.

Phenomena are interconnected to the extent that they are ultimately manifestations of the same underlying energy or life force. The principle of interconnectedness means that although there can be a vast number of variations upon a theme, there can essentially be only one underlying theme or energy source. Interconnectedness implies that we are empty of an inherently existing self. However, by default, it also implies that we are full of absolutely everything that exists. Therefore, if *emptiness* is a word that you are not completely comfortable with, you can simply exchange it for the word *fullness*. In emptiness there is fullness, and in fullness there is emptiness.

ANALYTICAL MEDITATION

Interconnectedness is a good way of thinking about emptiness because interconnectedness isn't a particularly difficult notion to understand. However, one of the downfalls of seeing emptiness through the lens of interconnectedness is that it introduces a number of "conceptual glitches" that are difficult to resolve using logic and reasoning. For example, by asserting that phenomena do not possess intrinsic existence because they are deeply interconnected, it overlooks the fact that in order for something to connect to something else, it must exist. If something doesn't exist, then there are no logical grounds for asserting that it can connect to another thing that also doesn't exist.

Thus, interconnectedness gets us halfway toward understanding the principle of emptiness, but to come to a fuller and more accurate understanding, we need to use interconnectedness up until a certain point and then let go of it. This process of making use of interconnectedness and then transcending it completely, can be practiced during analytical or insight meditation. You might recall that in chapter 4, we discussed the practice of concentrative meditation, which is used to steady and introduce tranquility into the mind. Analytical meditation should be practiced after a prior period of establishing oneself in meditative concentration, and it involves gathering the tranquility and attentional focus cultivated during concentrative meditation, and directing it in such a way that it 'penetrates' the truth of a particular subject. More specifically, what we are trying to do during analytical meditation is establish the true status of a given phenomenon in terms of whether it inherently exists (i.e., whether it has a 'self').

Thus, we allow the mind to settle and calm itself during concentrative meditation, and the next step is to choose a meditative object and search within it for the existence of something that can be called a "self." One of the best objects to meditatively investigate in this respect is actually ourselves (i.e., the human being). After we reach the point where we feel rooted in meditative calm, we remain aware of our breath, body, feelings, and thoughts, but we allow a part of our meditative awareness to start gently searching for the existence of a "me," a "mine," or an "I." We take ourselves as the object of meditation, and we commence a process of meditative investigation.

An example of an analytical meditation that can be used to investigate whether we intrinsically exist is as follows:

Breathing in, I observe that I have established myself in awareness of breathing;
Breathing out, I observe that I have established myself in awareness of being.
Breathing in, I observe that tranquility and concentration have arisen in the mind;
Breathing out, I bathe in this tranquility and concentration.
Breathing in, I begin the process of searching for a self;
Breathing out, I look deeply inside myself.

Breathing in, I discover blood, flesh, bone, organs, hair, teeth, and nails;
Breathing out, I do not find anything that can be called a self.
Breathing in, I discover clouds, rain, rivers, and oceans;
Breathing out, I do not find anything that can be called a self.
Breathing in, I discover plants, trees, insects, fish, and animals;
Breathing out, I do not find anything that can be called a self.
Breathing in, I discover my parents, grandparents, and all of my ancestors;
Breathing out, I do not find anything that can be called a self.
Breathing in, I discover the moon, sun, planets, and stars;
Breathing out, I do not find anything that can be called a self.
Breathing in, I discover all my thoughts, choices, words, and actions;
Breathing out, I do not find anything that can be called a self.
Breathing in, I discover that I am deeply interconnected to everything that exists;
Breathing out, I do not find anything that can be called a self.
Breathing in, I discover that since I am all things, I must relinquish the idea of being connected;
Breathing out, since I am unable to discover a self, I relinquish the idea that I intrinsically exist.

In the above meditation, the first four lines (i.e., the first two in- and out-breath exercises) denote the concluding part of a typical concentrative meditation exercise. The analytical meditation then begins at line five, where we start to look deeply inside ourselves. The idea with this meditation is to use observation and logical skills to come to the conclusion that we do not inherently exist. However, these observations and logical skills should be guided by intuition and spiritual intelligence, rather than intensive thinking or conceptualization. When this meditation is practiced properly, we create the correct conditions in the mind for meditative insights to arise organically. However, if we try to force them to arise, we will prevent them from doing so. The term *analytical meditation* sounds like it might require a lot of mental energy, but in actual fact, it is a very gentle (albeit delicate and subtle) practice.

LABELING THE SELF

In the above example analytical meditation, we searched for the existence of an inherently existing self within our component parts (e.g., bones, flesh, blood, etc.) and also within the various causes and conditions that are necessary for the body to manifest (e.g., the air that we breathe, water that we drink, our parents who reproduced in order for us to be born). If we take any one of these individual components or causes and try to locate our self-existence within them, it is obvious that we are not going to find it there. For example, we know that we don't exist as, or within, a single bone of the body, or in an apple that we are about to eat for lunch. We also know that our existence cannot be found outside the various causes and conditions that give rise to the body and mind. Based on these two observations (i.e., that we do not exist as each cause individually or external to these causes), a person might come to the conclusion that we exist as the sum product of all of the causes and conditions that cooperate in order for us to manifest.

Asserting that we exist as the sum of our parts might seem like a reasonable argument to make, but on closer examination, it becomes apparent that this assertion is also logically flawed. If we accept that we do not exist in each component part individually, but then assert that we exist as the sum of these parts, what we are effectively arguing is that when the component parts come together, they stop being component parts and become an entirely new entity. If we assert that the heart is a component of the body but when it's together with all other bodily components it should not be considered as a heart, then we are illogically asserting that the heart is actually two things at the same time (i.e., a component of the body on the one hand and something that is indistinguishable from all other aspects of the body on the other hand).

Given that component parts don't cease being component parts when they are assembled into a composite whole, by claiming that the body exists as the sum of its parts, we are actually positing that the body exists only as a name or label. For example, when a nib, cartridge, lid, and casing come together to form a pen, we don't say, *"Please can you pass me my nib, cartridge, lid, and casing that are all joined together?"* We simply ask them to pass the pen. However, the word *pen* simply refers to a collection of specific components that are assembled in a particular arrangement. The "pen" doesn't inherently exist, but is simply a label used to denote a specific arrangement of given components.

If we take some pieces of wood and assemble them in a certain manner, it is possible to construct something that is commonly referred to as a hut or shelter. However, if we take the exact same pieces of wood and assemble them in an alternative arrangement, then it is possible to construct any number of different objects that are known by other names (e.g., a bench, kennel, table, gazebo, window frame, roof, etc.). Each of these objects are made of exactly the same pieces of wood, but they have different labels. The "self" of these objects does not exist in each piece of wood individually, and it doesn't suddenly manifest when the individual pieces of wood are assembled together.

Returning to the example of the pen, if we examine an individual pen component such as the cartridge, we discover that it too, is just a label used to refer to a collection of particular components that are assembled in a certain manner (in this case ink and a small plastic or metal cylindrical container that houses the ink). If we try to find the "selfness" of the cartridge, all we come up with is a collection of components that do not contain the "selfness" of the cartridge either when they are separated, or when they are joined together. Thus, "emptiness of self" applies as much to "fully assembled" objects (such as a pen) as it does to their individual components (such as a cartridge), and to the various subcomponents that comprise these individual components (and so on).

Although it might be a difficult notion to accept, if we use logic and reasoning to investigate phenomena, then we are left with no alternative other than to conclude that in their ultimate aspect, phenomena exist only as labels. To help explain this notion a little further, the following is adapted from a short "think" piece that we wrote called "Dream or Reality?"[1] It is a dialogue between a professor and a student and shows how, through the use of deductive reasoning, it can be demonstrated that phenomena exist only as labels. The dialogue also demonstrates that it is impossible to definitively conclude that phenomena we perceive during waking reality are any more "real" than phenomena we perceive while asleep and dreaming.

Student: *Professor?*

Professor: *Yes.*

Student: *Pinch me.*

Professor: *What are you talking about?*

Student: *It's just that we've been testing the Shared Dream Inducer so frequently that I can't remember if I set the time on the Dream Termination Device.*

Professor: *I hope you're joking.*

Student: *No seriously, I know you've told me so many times but I just can't remember.*

Professor: *You mean . . .*

Student: *Yes, there's no way of knowing whether we're currently in a shared dream or in waking reality. If it turns out we're dreaming, the Shared Dream Inducer could keep us here indefinitely.*

Professor: *How shall we remedy this situation?*

Student: *We could just activate the Shared Dream Inducer and try to enter a dream via the brain-computer interface; if it allows us entry, then at least we'll know whether we're awake or dreaming.*

Professor: *That's way too risky. If we're already dreaming, we could end up getting stuck in a nested dream.*

Student: *OK, I have another idea. In a dream, everything is the product of the mind. Things appear real to the dreamer yet everything is an illusion.*

Professor: *Agreed. But what is your point?*

Student: *So all we have to do is choose some objects around us and work out if they truly exist. If they're real, then we're awake, otherwise we're dreaming.*

Professor: *Interesting idea. Here, you can start with my fountain pen.*

Student: *Well, the pen certainly writes when I put it to paper. Yes, I think it's real. I think we're awake.*

Professor: *So your criterion for existence is based on the function that an object performs?*

Student: *Yes, of course.*

Professor: *I see. Go ahead and take away all of the components of the pen so that you're left with nothing other than the nib. Does the nib still write?*

Student: *Yes, there is still a small amount of ink remaining in the nib. It still writes.*

Professor: *But the nib isn't the pen?*

Student: *Ah, good point. It appears my original premise was wrong. The nib is just a single pen component and cannot be all of the individual parts that comprise the pen. One thing cannot be another thing.*

Professor: *So is the pen real?*

Student: *Well, having just taken the pen apart and seen that all of its component parts are present, I would still conclude that it is real. I still think we're awake.*

Professor: *So you're saying that the pen exists as the sum of its component parts?*

Student: *Yes, that's right.*

Professor: *Ah, I see. But you've already said that a component part can't be two things at once. Yet now you seem to be saying that when the nib, cartridge, lid, and other pen components are put together, they stop being those components and become a new single entity?*

Student: *No, that is illogical. The component parts still exist in the pen but the word "pen" is used to designate the collection of individual components that collectively form a pen.*

Professor: *Right, so you're saying that the pen is just a label?*

Student: *Well, I guess so.*

Professor: *If the pen is just a label, then it doesn't inherently exist. So are you now saying that we're currently dreaming?*

Student: *I'm a bit confused. Irrespective of whether we are awake or dreaming, although things certainly appear, there is no logical basis upon which it can be said they truly exist.*

Professor: *Yes, that is correct. Therefore, your idea of investigating whether or not things are real doesn't get us any closer to working out whether we are currently dreaming or awake. Have you got any better ideas?*

Student: If we're currently shared dreaming, it means the Shared Dream Inducer is keeping some of our brainwave frequencies in perfect synchrony. We could try to disrupt them and wake ourselves up by inducing an electric shock.

Professor: If you want to stick your finger in the electric socket then go right ahead, but I'm certainly not joining you. Any more ideas?

Student: Hmm. Well I don't ever remember bursting into laughter during a dream. So why don't I tell you a funny joke and if it makes you laugh then that means we're not dreaming?

Professor: I'm not convinced about this suggestion. However, go ahead and tell your joke.

Student: What did the professor who always gave examples say when asked how many eggs they'd like for breakfast?

Professor: I don't know.

Student: Four eggs ample.

Professor: I thought you were going to make me laugh.

Student: Very funny.

Professor: Well if you haven't got any more sensible ideas, then I have a suggestion. Let's just stop, breathe, and do nothing.

Student: I don't understand.

Professor: I built a failsafe into the Shared Dream Inducer so that even if the Dream Termination Device isn't activated, the dream automatically terminates after eight hours.

Student: What! Couldn't you have told me that an hour ago?

Professor: Well, haven't you learned something?

Student: You're right, I've actually learned rather a lot. The dream occurs within the expanse of mind and in a dream, there is the impression of coming and going, yet nothing really moves. While dreaming, there is also near and far, but there is actually no distance. In a dream, although things appear, they are illusory and cannot be said to truly exist. However, objects perceived by the waking-state consciousness are also devoid of intrinsic existence. So are you saying that waking reality also unfolds within the expanse of mind?

Professor: You'll have to work that out for yourself.

Student: But we still haven't determined whether we're currently dreaming or awake?

Professor: Does it really matter? Can't you just relax and enjoy each moment of whichever reality you are currently in?

AWAKE OR DREAMING?

The professor-student dialogue highlights a key principle of emptiness. It demonstrates that although phenomena certainly appear and can be perceived, in their ultimate aspect, they have exactly the same properties of existence as dreamed images. The fact that we know phenomena are empty of a self but are able to perceive them should prevent us from falling into the trap of believing that emptiness means complete nothingness or non-existence. Likewise, the fact that we know phenomena are illusory (i.e., dream-like) in nature should prevent us from falling into the trap of rejecting the idea of emptiness and believing that phenomena exist in the absolute sense of the word.

As referred to earlier in this chapter, coming to the realization that phenomena are empty of inherent existence and dreamlike in nature, is something that we should allow to happen organically. It is a realization that the Mindful Warrior comes to gradually, and not something that they try to force or think too hard about. In fact, rather than engage in excessive thinking about emptiness and the illusory nature of existence, all we really have to do is open our eyes and observe what is happening directly in front of us.

For example, let's think about this exact instance in time. Presumably, you are reading these words from a paper book or electronic device. Either way, the present moment that you are experiencing in this instant of time (i.e., while reading this specific sentence) is different from the present moment that you experienced when you read the previous sentence. Based on this observation, it is reasonable to conclude that time is continuously passing and that the present moment is constantly changing.

However, although it is understandable that we might be under the impression that time is always passing and the present moment is continuously changing, this constitutes an erroneous perception of how time and the present moment actually operate. If we say that the present moment is always changing, it (obviously) implies that a process of change is in operation. For a moment of time to change into another moment of time, the first moment of time must completely manifest and crystalize into existence. However, time can be divided into infinitely smaller and smaller units. For example, a second can be divided by 1,000 to form a millisecond, and a millisecond can be further divided to form a microsecond (one millionth of a second). A microsecond can then be divided to form an attosecond (one quintillionth of a second), and an attosecond can be subsequently divided to form a yoctosecond (one septillionth of a second). However, even a yoctosecond—which is undoubtedly an incredibly brief period of time—can be divided again and again. Since a moment of time can always be divided into infinitely smaller moments of time, the idea that there is such a thing as a "fixed" moment in time is implausible.

In much the same way that it appears a river is always flowing, it appears that the present moment is in a constant state of motion. However, if something is continuously changing and never actually comes to rest in a fixed state, then how can it be said that it undergoes any kind of change? Change implies that something changes from one state or position to another. But since phenomena (including the present moment) never become truly static, it is technically inaccurate to say that they change. Something that never stops changing doesn't ever crystalize into existence, and as such, it can't be said to undergo change. In other words, there never has existed, and there will never exist, something that can be called a fixed instant of time in which all forms of change and motion have temporarily ceased.

The fact that the present moment never fully crystalizes into existence tells us that the present moment is of the nature of emptiness. It appears that certain scientific disciplines—particularly the field of quantum mechanics—are coming to the same conclusion. Indeed, many quantum theorists accept that at the subatomic level, there can never be absolute certainty that a particle exists at a given position in time or space. Recently, it has been demonstrated in an experimental setting that a minute metal blade of semiconductor material can be made to simultaneously vibrate in two different energy states.[2] This is the kinetic equivalent of matter being in two different places at the same time, and it demonstrates that at the subatomic level, particles can never be absolutely located in time and space (i.e., they exist nowhere and everywhere at the same time).

If we extend our hand and try to grasp the present moment, it slips straight through our fingers. We can look at the present moment, participate in the present moment, and enjoy it, but we can never really touch it or possess it. This is just like how a dream operates; we can perceive things in a dream, but we can never really own them. What we experience in a dream, no matter how marvelous and salubrious it might be, immediately collapses and vanishes as soon as we wake up. We believe the same thing happens when we die—the world and people that we knew start to permanently vanish from our perception.

The Mindful Warrior knows that the world that they perceive during waking reality bears much closer resemblance to a dream than popular opinion might suggest. In fact, perhaps the only major difference between waking reality and a dream is that in the case of the latter, the dreamed world is principally created and occupied by just one mind, whereas in the case of the former, it is created and occupied by many minds. Perhaps it is also the case that the more minds that occupy a world or reality, the more that world appears to be "real" and the more it has to follow physical rules. Conversely, when a reality is primarily created and occupied by just one mind (such as in a dream), then it is much easier to bend the rules of physics and to perform acts such as flying through the air or instantly changing one's location.

KNOWING THE RISKS

The nature of emptiness means that it is not the most easily comprehensible aspect of the Mindful Warrior's path to spiritual awakening. Therefore, although we have attempted to present our discussion of emptiness in a manner that is reasonably easy to understand, please don't worry if you have found the content of this chapter a little difficult to digest. If you revisit this chapter from time to time, then your understanding of emptiness should gradually improve. By understanding the key (so-called) "features" of emptiness, we can begin to look for signs of emptiness in our daily life as well as during meditation practice. In other words, developing a strong theoretical understanding of emptiness supports and strengthens our experiential understanding of emptiness (and vice versa). However, the truth is that emptiness is not something that can ever be fully "understood" using words and thoughts. We can formulate a reasonably good idea of what emptiness is about by reading books and listening to lectures, but emptiness is an experience and truth that transcends the limits of conceptual understanding. In fact, the more a person tries to define and compartmentalize emptiness, the further they will find themselves from the "essence" of emptiness.

Forming fixed concepts about emptiness is one of the main risks associated with this aspect of the Mindful Warrior's practice. There are a lot of intelligent scholars and meditation teachers (including Buddhist meditation teachers) who believe that they've got emptiness "nailed." They write lots of books and papers about it, and they make emptiness into an intellectual subject. But most of these people only have a very superficial or "academic" understanding of emptiness. In fact, a person who is not necessarily intelligent but just lives very simply and takes things one moment at a time, is probably situated much closer to emptiness than many of the clever scholars referred to above.

We're certainly not saying that it is a bad idea to think about or study emptiness, because doing so is an essential part of the meditative learning process. However, any study and investigation of emptiness should be undertaken with a full awareness of the limits of intellectual inquiry. Indeed, even a fully enlightened Mindful Warrior knows that there is always something more to learn about emptiness. An enlightened being might be able to dwell in emptiness at all times during the day and night, but this doesn't mean that there isn't room for them to refine their skills in terms of how to mold and work with the "fabric" and "energy" of emptiness (i.e., in order to create conditions that are conducive to others' spiritual awakening).

In addition to forming fixed concepts, a further risk associated with practicing emptiness is that the meditation practitioner may start to adopt a laissez-faire attitude toward life. People that fall into this trap often say things such as *"everything's empty, so what's the point in worrying about it"* or *"life is just a dream so chill out."* This type of attitude reflects a poor understanding of emptiness, and such people should not be considered as being suitable spiritual teachers or role models. The fact is that even where a spiritual practitioner has given rise to a full realization of emptiness, it is almost certain that the people whom they encounter and interact with on a day-to-day basis won't have done so. A person can be told one million times that reality lacks intrinsic existence, but unless they have awakened to this experience of their own accord, you can be 99.9 percent certain that emptiness will be the last thing on their mind when they find themselves in a difficult or distressing situation. In other words, it is unrealistic to expect people who are not walking an authentic spiritual path to understand emptiness, and it is even more unrealistic to expect them to find refuge and support in emptiness when they are facing adverse conditions.

Consequently, when the Mindful Warrior begins to reach the stage where they perceive and interact with the world through the lens of emptiness, they are incredibly aware of how their thoughts, words, and actions will influence others. The Mindful Warrior understands that even though suffering does not intrinsically exist (i.e., because it is made of the fabric of dreams), the person immersed in soap opera living experiences suffering as though it is 100 percent raw, real, and unremitting. Thus, rather than negate a spiritual practitioner's duty to act with consideration and compassion, the arising of an authentic understanding of emptiness exponentially increases the extent to which they are responsible for alleviating the suffering and ignorance of all living beings.

MAHAVAIRORCANA'S ONE MIND

We would like to conclude this chapter with a short four-verse (each of four lines) *vajragiti* that we wrote called "Mahavairocana's One Mind." The idea behind writing this *vajragiti* was to try to express in more intuitive (rather than logical or academic) terms what the notion of emptiness is all about. In Buddhism, Mahavairocana is considered to be the name of a great Buddha, but the term can also be used to denote the wider principle and qualities of the fully enlightened mind. Much like how Christianity expresses God through the principle of the Trinity (i.e., the Father, Son, and Holy Spirit), Buddhism expresses the principle of the fully enlightened mind (i.e., of Mahavairocana or of Buddhahood more generally) through the tripartite principle of the Dharmakaya, Sambhogakaya, and Nirmanakaya.

The Sanskrit suffix *kaya* means "body" and the prefixes *dharma*, *sambhoga*, and *nirmana* mean "truth," "enjoyment," and "manifest," respectively. If we want to draw parallels with the Christian tradition, then the Buddhist term *dharmakaya* might be likened to the Father. However, this link only remains valid where the term *Father* is understood to correspond to the emptiness that underlies (and is the "father" of) all that is (i.e., rather than an actual God being who is the creator of the universe). *Sambhogakaya* could be likened to the Holy Spirit, and it refers to the potential of the *dharmakaya* to express itself as energy. When a big bang happens and from complete emptiness a universe explodes into existence, this is an example of the *dharmakaya* expressing itself as energy. Another example would be when a fully enlightened being decides, for whatever reason, to temporarily appear (i.e., within the dream or mind of a discerning spiritual practitioner) as a body made of pure white light. The term *nirmanakaya* could be likened to the Son, referring to the ability of the enlightened mind to take form as (for example) a human being.

> *I am Mahavairocana, the one Mind,*
> *All things arise as me,*
> *I am the entirety of space and time,*
> *Yet you will not find me there.*
>
> *If you take now and all that occurs as the path,*
> *Allowing perceived and perceiver to merge as one,*
> *Seeing my face in all that unfolds,*
> *Then you forever enter my deathless realm.*
>
> *When you realize that throughout all lifetimes,*
> *There has never once been any coming or going,*
> *Nothing has ever been accomplished, nothing left undone,*
> *You perfect the three kayas in a single instant.*
>
> *With pristine mirror-like cognizance,*
> *Relax into the awareness of your intrinsic wakefulness,*
> *All things are Mind-born, yet don't search for that Mind,*

Noble one, you have been introduced!

Om Mahavairocana Hum

11

THE MINDFUL WARRIOR'S LINEAGE

We have now discussed mindfulness and all the main concepts and practices that are traditionally joined to it. The only thing that we have not discussed is how this knowledge is passed down to us, and where we should look to find support on the path of the Mindful Warrior.

A CHAIN OF TRANSMISSION

In contemporary Buddhism, and particularly within the West, people tend to place a lot of emphasis on lineage. The word *lineage* basically refers to the teaching ancestry of a particular spiritual practitioner or teacher. The idea is that there should be an unbroken chain of transmission that can be traced from a Buddhist teacher all the way back to the historical Buddha, or to another enlightened being. Therefore, in contemporary Buddhist culture, people tend to use lineage as a means of validating themselves as "authentic" spiritual teachers and of reassuring potential students that they are in safe (and spiritually inspired) hands.

Unfortunately, however, things aren't that simple, because although lineage can be a useful indication of an individual's "authority" to teach, it can also blind people as to the innermost qualities and intentions of the particular teacher they have placed their faith in. Today, there are numerous Buddhist teachers (lay and monastic) who can reel off a list of all their teachers, titles, and qualifications, and who can trace their teaching ancestry back to the historical Buddha (or another historic figure deemed to have attained enlightenment). However, the truth of the matter is that it is very rare to come across an authentic spiritual teacher (Buddhist or otherwise).

It seems that a Chinese Zen Buddhist teacher known as Huang Po made the same observation when he was alive some twelve hundred years ago. According to Huang Po's estimate, only five of every ten thousand meditation teachers and practitioners would meet his criteria for being an authentic spiritual practitioner. Huang Po provided this estimate during a time when, according to Buddhist thought, people placed much more importance on spiritual teachings and values.

Certain Buddhist texts divide history into different time epochs, and these epochs basically correspond to the "state of health" of the spiritual teachings during that particular period of time. For example, when Huang Po was alive and teaching approximately twelve hundred years ago, this was known as the Age of Semblance Dharma (Sanskrit: *pratirupadharma*, Japanese: *zō bō*). The Age of Semblance Dharma was a period when it was reasonably easy to find a semblance of the authentic spiritual teachings, but if you wanted to find something more meaningful and profound, then you would have to search very hard. The Age of Semblance Dharma came after an epoch known as The Age of True Law (Sanskrit: *saddharma*, Japanese: *shōbō*), which was a period when the spiritual teachings were in a much better state of health (this earlier epoch also covered the period when the historical Buddha lived and taught, some twenty-five hundred years ago).

The epoch of time that we are currently in is known as The Latter Day of The Law or the Age of Degeneration of the Dharma (Sanskrit: *pashchimadharma*, Japenese: *mappō*), and it corresponds to a period of widespread demise of the spiritual teachings.

Therefore, given that Huang Po's aforementioned estimate was made at a time when the spiritual teachings were deemed to be in a much healthier condition, if we were to try and calculate the number of spiritual teachers and practitioners alive today who are truly living and breathing their practice, it is probable that the result would be significantly less than Huang Po's approximation. Encountering an authentic spiritual teacher is a very rare and precious happening, and if we are fortunate to meet such an individual, then we should make the most of the opportunity.

We have personally been ordained within, or received spiritual transmissions from, numerous Buddhist lineages. We have been ordained as Buddhist monks in Mahayana Buddhist traditions and yogic (i.e., tantric) Buddhist traditions, and we have also received the higher ordination in the Theravada Buddhist tradition. We have had lots of spiritual teachers, and we have tremendous and heartfelt respect for all of them. However, simply because a teacher was taught or ordained by a recognized lineage holder, this does not automatically mean that they have fully absorbed, embodied, and realized all that their predecessor had to offer. This is what the Buddha's close disciple Ananda said (as recorded in the *Sandaka Sutta*[1]) about the risks associated with relying too much on traditions and lineages:

> Here some teacher is a traditionalist, one who regards oral tradition as truth, he teaches a *Dharma* by oral tradition, by legends handed down, by the authority of the collections. But when a teacher is a traditionalist, one who regards oral tradition as truth, some is well transmitted and some badly transmitted, some is true and some is otherwise.

THE MINDFUL WARRIOR'S TEACHER

We are certainly not saying that lineage isn't important. It is beautiful that there exist Buddhist (and other spiritual) traditions that are thousands of years old and that take pride in their lineage history. However, as aspiring Mindful Warriors, we have to be intelligent and cautious about whom we adopt as a spiritual teacher, and we have to understand the various qualities that make a good teacher.

You sometimes hear of people who have followed the advice and inspiration of a particular teacher for many years but who immediately withdraw their respect and devotion when they hear the slightest rumor or bad report about their teacher. In all probability, such people placed faith in their teacher because of factors such as the teacher's popularity, charisma, lineage, and/or qualifications.

The aspiring Mindful Warrior knows what to look for in a potential spiritual teacher, and they place their trust in a teacher because they experience directly that the teacher has given rise to authentic spiritual realization. By the term *experience directly*, we mean that the wisdom and compassion of the teacher profoundly touches the heart and mind of the aspiring Mindful Warrior. An authentic spiritual teacher might be quietly reading, eating, or gardening, but in their presence, one should automatically begin to feel calm and spiritually inspired.

If we enter into a spiritual relationship with a teacher because of their qualities of transcendent wisdom and compassion, then we know, through direct experience, that the teacher has allowed the wisdom of emptiness to flourish in their mind. This wisdom supports, nourishes, and guides us at all times. In the presence of an authentic spiritual teacher, with each breath we take, we make huge strides forward on the path of the Mindful Warrior. A spiritually realized teacher warrants our respect, love, and devotion at all times, and if we approach and relate to them with the right attitude, they will quickly guide us out of the mire of soap opera living.

If we are sincere and true in our intentions to walk the path of the Mindful Warrior, then we will maximize our chances of meeting an authentic spiritual guide. It is best if we don't have fixed or predetermined ideas as to what a spiritual teacher should look like or of what their role in society should be. They might be a person who has spent decades in monasteries or who is actively giving *Dharma* talks and writing books about spiritual practice. However, they may have followed a different direction in life and might be a parent, solicitor, shop keeper, business professional, cleaner, or musician. The authentic spiritual teacher might be rich or poor, young or old, in good health or bad health. They might be a man or woman, and they may or may not have studied at university.

Although spiritual teachers can come in many different shapes and sizes, there are some inner qualities that should be present in the teacher. First and foremost, they should be free of attachment to wealth, reputation, and pleasure (or anything else for that matter). This isn't to say that the spiritual teacher can't enjoy comfortable surroundings and pleasurable experiences, but they should be perfectly happy and willing to walk away from such favorable conditions if and when the need arises. In the face of adverse conditions or imminent danger, the spiritual teacher should remain centered and calm. In such situations decisive action and a quick response might be required, but the spiritual teacher shouldn't panic or lose their meditative awareness. They should have a serene and disciplined mind that is free of the slightest taint of fear, hatred, or anger. The spiritual teacher should be skilled at "directly seeing" and guiding the minds of those who have chosen to walk with them on the path to liberation.

If we are putting into practice the teachings of an authentic spiritual guide, then genuine spiritual experiences should begin to arise in the mind. If we have been practicing with the teacher for a period of many years and such spiritual experiences have not arisen, then it is either because the teacher is not suitably skilled, or because our attitude is preventing us from fully assimilating their teachings. An authentic spiritual teacher emanates mindful awareness, presence, and joy. They have limitless compassion and are skilled at relating to, and working with, the minds of people from many different walks in life. In the company of an accomplished spiritual teacher, people become healthier, happier, and calmer, and even animals enjoy being in their presence.

Perhaps the best way for the aspiring Mindful Warrior to consider their relationship with their spiritual teacher is as their closest and most trusted friend. However, the depth of the relationship extends far beyond this because assuming our spiritual journey continues beyond death, the friendship with an authentic spiritual teacher doesn't just last for this lifetime.

As the aspiring Mindful Warrior's friendship with their spiritual teacher continues to grow, a kind of transference starts to take place. The spiritual teacher waters and nourishes the wisdom inside us, and by giving us a taste of their own wisdom, they help us to locate and connect with our own enlightened nature. After the relationship with the authentic spiritual teacher has become firmly cemented, it is less important to be in close proximity to them. A spiritual bond is created, which means that even if we find ourselves on opposite sides of the earth, we are still very much in the teacher's presence. This is what the twelfth-century Tibetan Buddhist Saint Gampopa said about meeting the teacher without necessarily being in their presence:

> In the future, those who think, "Alas, I haven't met [Gampopa]" should simply study and practice the texts that I composed. . . . There is no particle of difference; it is the same as meeting me. Those who are having a hard time understanding and practicing the *Dharma*, think of me and supplicate with devotion. The blessings will arise naturally.[2]

THE NATURAL LINEAGE OF ALL THAT IS

If we spend time in the company (whether physical or "spiritual") of an authentic spiritual teacher, and if we are diligent in our practice, then the lineage of the teacher will be gradually conferred upon us. We are not talking here about the teacher guiding us through a long list of teachings, rituals, and spiritual techniques that were passed down to them from their teacher. Indeed, a lot of contemporary Buddhist and meditation traditions regard lineage

transmission in the same way as training for an academic or professional qualification. However, true lineage transmission is an
entirely individual process and isn't about filling another person's
mind up with copious amounts of information and teachings.
Rather, it's about uncluttering the mind of its attachments, concepts, and preconceived ideas.

When an authentic spiritual teacher shares their lineage with
another person, they are simply introducing the person to the
spiritual lineage that is already present inside them. Ultimately,
this "natural" lineage is the only lineage that counts. It is the same
lineage that every enlightened being who has ever walked this
earth belongs to, and it is the same lineage that everybody who
attains enlightenment in the future will awake to. If you read
books about Buddhism and meditation, you will probably find references to numerous different types of practice lineages. However, really and truly, there is only one spiritual lineage. Jesus Christ,
the Buddha, and all spiritually inspired leaders belong to this lineage, and so does everybody walking the path of the Mindful Warri-
or.

To progress further on the path, it is essential to make contact
with an authentic spiritual guide. However, until this happens, any
aspiring Mindful Warrior can begin to tap into the natural lineage
that exists inside them. When we practice breathing in and out in
awareness, and when we are dwelling in the here and now, then
we encounter this self-existing lineage. In this manner, calmness
and spiritual presence are conferred upon us by ourselves. By
having a pure and sincere intention to break free of soap-opera
living, we automatically join, and receive the blessings of, the lineage of the Mindful Warriors. From this point of view, we are our
own teacher, and the present moment is our training ground.

The lineage of the Mindful Warriors is a very ancient lineage. It
existed well before the time of the historical Buddha, and it will
exist for long after the dissolution of this planet. It is a lineage that
has existed since before the beginning of time. The lineage of the
Mindful Warriors can't be owned and it doesn't belong to anybody. It pervades every moment of time, every atomic and sub-

atomic particle, and every single square inch of known and unknown space. It is the birth right of every living being on the
planet to tap into, and become a holder of, this natural and all-
pervasive lineage. People need only to decide that they wish to
embrace and be nourished by the spiritual lineage that exists within all things. We either choose to live life in awareness and use this
precious human life to work toward enlightenment, or we choose
to remain caught in a soap opera.

As far as making genuine spiritual progress is concerned, there
unfortunately isn't any room for indecision. A person needs to
decide whether they are "in," or whether they are "out." There
isn't any room for fence-sitters on the path of the Mindful Warriors. It would be easy to think that you could dabble in spiritual
development, practice meditation when it is convenient, and put
spiritual practice to one side when there are other things to do.
However, we are sorry to say so, but there is no middle ground. A
person either does their best to live their life through the practice
of spiritual awareness, or they turn their back on it.

For those who choose to dedicate their life to spiritual growth,
they will encounter and be nourished by a boundless well of wisdom, peace, and spiritual joy. Such aspiring Mindful Warriors will
remain as "individuals," but they will also be joined as "one." They
will become "one" by forming part of the family of the Mindful
Warriors whose love for one another is so profound, that it allows
such beings to breathe in harmony and unison with each other,
and with the universe.

LINEAGE BROTHERS AND SISTERS

In this chapter, we have made reference to a lineage that can be
accessed by anybody who is resolute and sincere in their spiritual
intentions. In the same vein, we have also said that both Jesus
Christ and the Buddha (and for that matter any other historic
enlightened being) also belong to this lineage. It's not just us who

have this view because, as recorded in the Gospel of St. Thomas, this was also the view of Jesus Christ:

> Jesus said: If those who lead you say to you "look, the kingdom is in the sky," then the birds of the sky will precede you. If they say to you, "It is in the sea," then the fish will precede you. Rather, the kingdom is inside of you, and it is outside of you. When you come to know yourselves, then you will become known, and you will realize that it is you who are the sons of the living Father. But if you will not know yourselves, you dwell in poverty and it is you who are that poverty.

12

DO YOU KNOW WHO I AM?

Throughout this book we have introduced and discussed the way of the Mindful Warrior. The purpose of doing so is to try to present a fresh and authoritative account of what it really means to practice mindfulness. Today, there are so many new mindfulness courses being offered, and so much is being written about mindfulness, that it is becoming increasingly difficult for people to discover authentic spiritual teachings. Consequently, words such as *McMindfulness* have been coined and circulated across the internet. It is important that care and caution are employed when choosing whether to practice with a given mindfulness or spiritual teacher. However, we shouldn't be dissuaded from practicing mindfulness and embracing it as a way of life.

It is really great that modern science has taken an interest in mindfulness and that there is a growing evidence base demonstrating that mindfulness leads to improvements in (among other things) health and psychosocial functioning. However, as far as the 2,500-year-old Buddhist tradition (and certain remits of other spiritual traditions) is concerned, this research doesn't really tell us anything we didn't already know. Mindfulness has worked for the last 2,500 years, and it will work for the next 2,500 years. Anybody who truly embraces mindfulness and practices it correctly will derive real benefits to their physical, psychological, and (most importantly) spiritual wellbeing.

As we outlined at the very start of this book, the purpose behind delineating the path of the Mindful Warrior was to cut through the hype and superficiality that has been created around mindfulness, in order to return to the spiritual essence of this important aspect of Buddhist practice. Mindfulness is a highly effective and expedient means of progressing along the spiritual path. From the point of view of spiritual development, we believe that a single minute spent being fully aware of the present moment is more potent than an entire decade spent studying Buddhist (or other spiritual) scriptures. The path of the Mindful Warrior is a complete and authentic spiritual path. It can lead to full spiritual awakening, including within a single lifetime.

However, it is a path for the few rather than the many. The reason we say that it is a path for the few has nothing to do with it being a difficult path. Rather, by saying this we are highlighting the fact that in modern society, it seems that fewer and fewer people have the motivation and courage to break free of soap opera living. Walking the path of the Mindful Warrior is not a particularly difficult thing to do, but it requires absolute conviction in one's choices as well as a willingness to live life as a spiritual practice.

People have a tendency to think that walking a spiritual path means having to go without, or having to reject enjoyable experiences. However, such a presumption could not be further from the truth. When a person truly devotes themselves to spiritual practice, life becomes full and complete. The Mindful Warrior doesn't need to hold themselves back, or suppress the natural desire to taste the world and enjoy all that it has to offer. Regardless of whether it is a pleasurable or unpleasurable experience, the Mindful Warrior simply has to learn not to become attached to the various objects, people, and situations that they encounter. Remaining unattached to internal and external experiences is actually the only way to fully enjoy life. Attachment leads to suffering, and gradually drags us back into the realm of soap opera living. We can delight in the present moment, dance with it, and play with it. But if we try to grasp the present moment and own it, not only does it slip through our fingers, but our fingers get burned in the process.

The path of the Mindful Warrior is all about fully immersing oneself in the present moment without holding onto it. An accomplished Mindful Warrior is somebody who has perfected the art of letting go. Included within the range of experiences, objects, and concepts that the Mindful Warrior should seek to let go of, is the path of mindful warriorship itself. The Mindful Warrior walks this path with absolute focus, unremitting courage, and joyful perseverance. However, they are not attached to the idea of walking a path, nor even of being a Mindful Warrior.

We would like to conclude this chapter and book with a contemplative piece that we wrote called "Do You Know Who I Am?" We feel that this contemplative work makes reference to, and pulls together, all of the various aspects of mindful warriorship that have been discussed in this book.

I am not interested in where you have been or what you have done.
I care not who you are, but I care deeply how you are.
If you are happy—truly happy—then so am I.
Do you know who I am?

You could be rich or poor, young or old, educated or uneducated, a man or woman.
You could be successful or unsuccessful, of high status or low status, a sinner or saint.
All of these things are irrelevant to me.
Do you know who I am?

I care not what religion you belong to.
I also do not care if you abstain from religion altogether.
What I represent transcends the beliefs, rituals, and concepts of any religion.
Do you know who I am?

In so far as I have an objective, it is to help you to help yourself.
In this regard, I prefer to be gentle and kind with you.

But I can also be incredibly firm and unyielding, if it will benefit you.
Do you know who I am?

I am flexible and can be whoever you need me to be to help you.
But you must always strive to be who I am, I cannot be who you are.
This is a matter about which I am inflexible.
Do you know who I am?

I feel happy when I see kindness in others.
I feel sad when I see cruelty in others.
But I am not attached to any of my feelings.
Do you know who I am?

I see praise and criticism as the same thing.
Because I know myself, it matters not what others say or think about me.
My happiness is unconditional.
Do you know who I am?

The faithless and cowardly see me as a charlatan.
They perceive everything through the lens of ignorance, fear, and selfishness.
But the pure in heart are drawn to me and are nourished by my presence.
Do you know who I am?

I have walked with kings and beggars, lived in poverty and luxury.
But these things make no difference to me.
Whatever my circumstances, I always live simply and am content.
Do you know who I am?

There are some with undisciplined minds that pretend to be me.
Interested only in being seen to do the right thing, they deceive their followers.
In my presence such impostors become angry, confused, and full of fear.
Do you know who I am?

Most people only start to think of me when they are dying.
But by waiting until then, it is difficult for me to help them.
I have always taught that the right time to get to know me is right now.
Do you know who I am?

Some people try to know me by looking outside of themselves.
They label me, box me with concepts, and worship me.
But I can never be known in this way.
Do you know who I am?

I exist within you and within all things.
Look deeply inside yourself and you will see me there.
You can be me if you really want to.
Do you know who I am?

To me, life and death are one and the same.
I am never really born, and I never really die.
You can be like this too if you want to.
Do you know who I am?

At all times, I am sustained by a spring of deep calm and joy.
I do not attach myself to anything, and my mind is completely unobstructed.
I soar freely and gracefully beyond the limits of space and time.
Do you know who I am?

I am the Mindful Warrior that resides within each and every one of you. I am waiting for you to awaken me and let me out before I perish in a world of benign ordinariness. If you help me, I, in turn, will help you. If you search within yourself, it won't take long to find me. Once you have found me, I will stay with you forever, even beyond death. At the point that you awaken me, a beacon of light will be lit inside of you. Your pure and compassionate presence will shine brighter than the sun, and shed light into the dark corners of people's hearts and minds. Tremors from your awakening will spread throughout the universe, and you will come to be known by many names. You will take your rightful place on the Dharma throne of the ancient Mindful Warriors. Search inside of yourself for me now. I am waiting.

BIBLIOGRAPHY

Bodhi, B. 2000. *The Connected Discourses of the Buddha: A New Translation of the Samyutta Nik ā ya*. Somerville, MA: Wisdom Publications.

Buddharakkhita. 1986. *Dhammapada: A Practical Guide to Right Living*. Bangalore: Maha Bodhi Society.

Chah, A. 2011. *The Collected Teachings of Ajahn Chah*. Belsay, UK: Aruna Publications.

Dalai Lama. 2001. *Stages of Meditation: Training the Mind for Wisdom*. London: Rider.

Dalai Lama, and A. Berzin. 1997. *The Gelug/Kagyu Tradition of Mahamudra*. New York: Snow Lion Publications.

de Lisle, S. M., N. A. Dowling, and J. S. Allen. 2012. "Mindfulness and Problem Gambling: A Review of the Literature." *Journal of Gambling Studies* 28: 719–39.

Digital Sanskrit Buddhist Canon. 2014. http://www.dsbcproject.org/.

Dorjee, D. 2010. "Kinds and Dimensions of Mindfulness: Why It Is Important to Distinguish Them." *Mindfulness* 1: 152–60.

Dudjom, K. 2005. *Wisdom Nectar. Dudjom Rinpoche's Heart Advice*. New York: Snow Lion Publications.

Eberth, J., and P. Sedlmeier. 2012. "The Effects of Mindfulness Meditation: A Meta-analysis." *Mindfulness* 3: 174–89.

Fjorback, L. O., M. Arendt, E. Ørnbøl, P. Fink, and H. Walach. 2011. "Mindfulness-Based Stress Reduction and Mindfulness-Based Cognitive Therapy: A Systematic Review of Randomized Controlled Trials." *Acta Psychiatrica Scandinavica* 124: 102–19.

Galante, J., I. Galante, M. Bekkers, and J. Gallacher, J. 2014. "Effect of Kindness-Based Meditation on Health and Well-Being: A Systematic Review and Meta-analysis." *Journal of Consulting and Clinical Psychology* 82: 1101–14.

Gampopa. 1998. *The Jewel Ornament of Liberation: The Wish-Fulfilling Gem of the Noble Teachings*. New York: Snow Lion Publications.

Gethin, R. 2011. "On Some Definitions of Mindfulness." *Contemporary Buddhism*, 12: 263–79.

Henke, M., and A. Chur-Hansen. 2014. "The Effectiveness of Mindfulness-Based Programs on Physical Symptoms and Psychological Distress in Patients with Fibromyalgia: A Systematic Review." *International Journal of Wellbeing* 4: 28–45.

Huang Po. 1982. *The Zen Teaching of Huang Po: On the Transmission of the Mind.* Translated by J. Blofeld. New York: Grove Press.

Kabat-Zinn, J. 1994. *Wherever You Go, There You Are: Mindfulness Meditation in Everyday Life.* New York: Hyperion.

Khyentse, D. 2007. *The Heart of Compassion: The Thirty-Seven Verses on the Practice of a Bodhisattva.* London: Shambhala.

Kuijpers, H., F. van der Heijden, S. Tuinier, and W. Verhoeven. 2007. "Meditation-Induced Psychosis." *Psychopathology* 40: 461–64.

Langhorst, J., P. Klose, G. J. Dobos, K. Bernardy, and W. Häuser. 2013. "Efficacy and Safety of Meditative Movement Therapies in Fibromyalgia Syndrome: A Systematic Review and Meta-analysis of Randomized Controlled Trials." *Rheumatology International* 33: 193–207.

Lutz, A., J. Brefczynski-Lewis, T. Johnstone, and R. Davidson. 2008. "Regulation of the Neural Circuitry of Emotion by Compassion Meditation: Effects of the Meditative Expertise." *PLoS ONE* 3: e1897. doi:10.1371/journal.pone.0001897

Manocha, R., D. Black, J. Sarris, and C. Stough. 2011. "A Randomised Controlled Trial of Meditation for Work Stress, Anxiety and Depressed Mood in Full-Time Workers." *Evidence-Based Complementary and Alternative Medicine*, Article ID 960583. doi:10.1155/2011/960583

Marlatt, A. G. 2002. "Buddhist Philosophy and the Treatment of Addictive Behaviours." *Cognitive and Behavioral Practice* 9: 44–50.

McWilliams, S. 2014. "Foundations of Mindfulness and Contemplation: Traditional and Contemporary Perspectives." *International Journal of Mental Health and Addiction* 12: 116–28.

Mental Health Foundation. 2010. *Mindfulness Report.* London: Author.

Milarepa. 1999. *The Hundred Thousand Songs of Milarepa: The Life-Story and Teaching of the Greatest Poet-Saint Ever to Appear in the History of Buddhism.* Translated by G. Chang. Boston: Shambhala Publications.

Monteiro, L. M., R. F. Musten, and J. Compson. 2015. "Traditional and Contemporary Mindfulness: Finding the Middle Path in the Tangle of Concerns." *Mindfulness* 6: 1–13.

Nagarjuna. 1995. *The Funadamental Wisdom of the Middle Way: Nāgārjuna's Mūlamadhyamakakārikā.* Translated by J. L. Garfield. New York: Oxford University Press.

Ñanamoli, B. 1979. *The Path of Purification: Visuddhi Magga.* Kandy, Sri Lanka: Buddhist Publication Society.

Ñanamoli, B., and B. Bodhi, trans. 2009. *Majjhima Nik ā ya: The Middle Length Discourses of the Buddha.* Fourth edition. Somerville, MA: Wisdom Publications.

Norbu, C., and A. Clemente. 1999. *The Supreme Source. The Fundamental Tantra of the Dzogchen Semde.* New York: Snow Lion Publications.

Nyanaponika Thera. 1983. *The Heart of Buddhist Meditation.* London: Rider.

O'Connell, A. D., M. Hofheinz, M. Ansmann, R. C. Bialczak, M. Lenander, E. Lucero, . . . and A. N. Cleland. 2010. "Quantum Ground State and Single-Phonon Control of a Mechanical Resonator." *Nature* 464: 697–703.

Ortiz de Gotari, A., K. Aronnson, and M. D. Griffiths. 2012. "Game Transfer Phenomena in Video Game Playing: A Qualitative Interview Study." *International Journal of Cyber Behavior, Psychology and Learning* 1: 15–33.

Perez-De-Albeniz, A., and J. Holmes. 2000. "Meditation: Concepts, Effects and Uses in Therapy." *International Journal of Psychotherapy* 5: 49–59.

Reat, N. 1993. *The Shalistamba Sutra.* Dehli: Molital Baranasidas.

Reddy, S., L. Negi, B. Dodson-Lavelle, B. Ozawa-de Silva, T. Pace, S. Cole, S., . . . and L. Craighead, L. 2013. "Cognitive-Based Compassion Training: A Promising

Prevention Strategy for At-Risk Adolescents." *Journal of Child and Family Studies* 22: 219–30.

Rhead, J. C., and G. G. May. 1983. "Meditation in a Specialized Correctional Setting: A Controlled Study." *Corrective and Social Psychiatry and Journal of Behaviour Technology Methods and Therapy* 29: 105–11.

Rhys Davids, T. 1881. *Buddhist Suttas*. Oxford: Clarendon Press.

Riley, B. 2014. "Experiential Avoidance Mediates the Association between Thought Suppression and Mindfulness with Problem Gambling." *Journal of Gambling Studies* 30: 163–71.

Robinson, B. 1998. "The Workaholic Family." *The American Journal of Family Therapy* 26: 65–75.

Rosch, E. 2007. "More Than Mindfulness: When You Have a Tiger by the Tail, Let It Eat You." *Psychological Inquiry* 18: 258–64.

Rosenberg, M. 1979. *Conceiving the Self*. New York: Basic Books.

Rungreangkulkji, S., W. Wongtakee, and S. Thongyot. 2011. "Buddhist Group Therapy for Diabetes Patients with Depressive Symptoms." *Archives of Psychiatric Nursing* 25: 195–205.

Santideva. 1997. *A Guide to the Bodhisattva Way of Life*. Translated by V. A. Wallace and A. B. Wallace. New York: Snow Lion Publications.

Shonin, E., and W. Van Gordon. 2013. "The Consuming Mind." *Mindfulness* 5: 345–47.

———. 2013. "Searching for the Present Moment." *Mindfulness* 5: 105–7.

———. 2014. "Mindfulness of Death." *Mindfulness* 5: 464–66.

———. 2014. "Using Mindfulness and Insight to Transform Loneliness." *Mindfulness* 5: 771–73.

———. 2015. "Practical Recommendations for Teaching Mindfulness Effectively." *Mindfulness* 6: 952–55.

———. 2015. "The Lineage of Mindfulness." *Mindfulness* 6: 141–45.

———. 2015. "Managers' Experiences of Meditation Awareness Training." *Mindfulness* 4: 899–909.

Shonin, E., W. Van Gordon, A. Compare, M. Zangeneh, and M. D. Griffiths. 2015. "Buddhist-Derived Loving-Kindness and Compassion Meditation for the Treatment of Psychopathology: A Systematic Review." *Mindfulness* 6: 1161–80.

Shonin, E., W. Van Gordon, T. Dunn, N. Singh, and M. D. Griffiths. 2014. "Meditation Awareness Training for Work-Related Wellbeing and Job Performance: A Randomized Controlled Trial." *International Journal of Mental Health and Addiction* 12: 806–23.

Shonin, E., W. Van Gordon, and M. D. Griffiths. 2013. "Buddhist Philosophy for the Treatment of Problem Gambling." *Journal of Behavioural Addictions* 2: 63–71.

———. 2013. "Mindfulness-Based Interventions: Towards Mindful Clinical Integration." *Frontiers in Psychology* 4: 194. DOI:10.3389/fpsyg.2013.00194.

———. 2014. "Cognitive Behavioral Therapy (CBT) and Meditation Awareness Training (MAT) for the Treatment Of Co-occurring Schizophrenia with Pathological Gambling: A Case Study." *International Journal of Mental Health and Addictions* 12: 181–96.

———. 2014. "Do Mindfulness-Based Therapies Have a Role in the Treatment of Psychosis?" *Australia and New Zealand Journal of Psychiatry* 48: 124–27.

———. 2014. "The Emerging Role of Buddhism in Clinical Psychology: Toward Effective Integration." *Psychology of Religion and Spirituality* 6: 123–37.

———. 2014. "Meditation Awareness Training (MAT) for Improved Psychological Wellbeing: A Qualitative Examination of Participant Experiences." *Journal of Religion and Health* 53: 849–63.

————. 2014. "Practical Tips for Teaching Mindfulness to School-Aged Children." *Education and Health* 32: 30–33.

————. 2014. "Practical Tips for Using Mindfulness in General Practice." *British Journal of General Practice* 64: 368–69.

————. 2014. "The Treatment of Workaholism with Meditation Awareness Training: A Case Study." *Explore: The Journal of Science and Healing* 10: 193–95.

————. 2015. "Mindfulness in Psychology: A Breath of Fresh Air?" *The Psychologist* 28: 28–31.

Shonin, E., W. Van Gordon, N. N. Singh, and M. D. Griffiths. 2015. "Mindfulness of Emptiness and the Emptiness of Mindfulness." In: *Buddhist Foundations of Mindfulness*, edited by E. Shonin, W. Van Gordon, and N. N. Singh, 159–78. New York: Springer.

Singh, N. N., G. E. Lancioni, A. S. W. Winton, B. T. Karazsia, and J. Singh. 2013. "Mindfulness Training for Teachers Changes the Behavior of Their Preschool Students." *Research in Human Development* 10: 211–33.

————. 2014. "Mindfulness-Based Positive Behavior Support (MBPBS) for Mothers of Adolescents with Autism Spectrum Disorders: Effects on Adolescents' Behavior and Parental Stress." *Mindfulness* 5: 646–57.

Singh, N. N., G. E. Lancioni, A. S. Winton, A. N. Singh, A. D. Adkins, and J. Singh. 2011. "Can Adult Offenders with Intellectual Disabilities Use Mindfulness-Based Procedures to Control Their Deviant Sexual Arousal?" *Psychology, Crime and Law* 17: 165–79.

Suzuki, D. 1983. *Manual of Zen Buddhism*. London: Rider.

Toneatto, T., L. Vettese, and L. Nguyen, L. 2007. "The Role of Mindfulness in the Cognitive-Behavioural Treatment of Problem Gambling." *Journal of Gambling Issues* 19: 91–101.

Trungpa, C. 2003. *The Collected Works of Chogyam Trungpa: Volume Four*. Boston: Shambhala.

Tsong-Kha-pa. 2004. *The Great Treatise on the Stages of the Path to Enlightenment* (Vol. 1). Edited by J. W. Cutler and G. Newland. Translated by the Lamrim Chenmo Translation Committee. New York: Snow Lion Publications.

Van Gordon, W., and M. D. Griffiths. 2015. "For the Mindful Teaching of Mindfulness." *The Psychologist* 28: 514–19. https://thepsychologist.bps.org.uk/volume-28/july-2015/mindful-teaching-mindfulness.

Van Gordon, W., E. Shonin, and M. Griffiths, M. 2015. "Toward a Second-Generation of Mindfulness-Based Interventions." *Australia and New Zealand Journal of Psychiatry* 49: 591–91.

Van Gordon, W., E. Shonin, M. D. Griffiths, and N. N. Singh. 2015. "Mindfulness and the Four Noble Truths." In *Buddhist Foundations of Mindfulness*, edited by E. Shonin, W. Van Gordon, and N. N. Singh, 9–27. New York: Springer.

————. 2015. "There Is Only One Mindfulness: Why Science and Buddhism Need to Work Together." *Mindfulness* 6: 49–56.

Van Gordon, W., E. Shonin, A. Sumich, E. Sundin, and M. D. Griffiths. 2013. "Meditation Awareness Training (MAT) for Psychological Wellbeing in a Sub-clinical Sample of University Students: A Controlled Pilot Study." *Mindfulness* 5: 381–91.

Van Gordon, W., E. Shonin, M. Zangeneh, and M. D. Griffiths. 2014. "Work-Related Mental Health and Job Performance: Can Mindfulness Help?" *International Journal of Mental Health and Addiction* 12: 129–37.

Walshe, M., trans. 1995. *The Long Discourses of the Buddha: A Translation of the Digha Nik ā ya*. Boston: Wisdom Publications.

NOTES

1. ALLOWING THE MIND TO BREATHE

1. The full findings of the research study are reported in the following publication: E. Shonin and W. Van Gordon, "Managers' Experiences of Meditation Awareness Training," *Mindfulness* 6 (2015): 899–909.

3. THE MINDFUL WARRIOR'S CODE

1. Examples of the studies that we are referring to are: N. N. Singh, et al., "Mindfulness-Based Positive Behavior Support (MBPBS) for Mothers of Adolescents with Autism Spectrum Disorders: Effects on Adolescents' Behavior and Parental Stress," *Mindfulness* 5 (2014): 646–57; and N. N. Singh et al., "Mindfulness Training for Teachers Changes the Behavior of Their Preschool Students," *Research in Human Development* 10 (2013): 211–33.

4. CARRY YOUR MEDITATION CUSHION WITH YOU

1. See E. Shonin, W. Van Gordon, and M. D. Griffiths, "Cognitive Behavioral Therapy (CBT) and Meditation Awareness Training (MAT)

for the Treatment of Co-occurring Schizophrenia with Pathological Gambling: A Case Study," *International Journal of Mental Health and Addiction* 12 (2014): 181–96; and E. Shonin, W. Van Gordon, and M. D. Griffiths, "The Treatment of Workaholism with Meditation Awareness Training: A Case Study," *Explore: The Journal of Science and Healing* 10 (2014): 193–95.

2. E. Shonin, " The Offspring of Spring," in *Candlelit Thoughts: A Collection of Poetry*. Peterborough: Forward Poetry.

5. A SPIRITUAL AFFAIR

1. For a detailed explanation of this definition and how it differs from other definitions of mindfulness, see W. Van Gordon, E. Shonin, and M. Griffiths, "Towards a Second-Generation of Mindfulness-Based Interventions," *Australia and New Zealand Journal of Psychiatry* 49 (2015): 591. Available at: http://anp.sagepub.com/content/49/7/591.full.

2. The *Ānāpānasati Sutta* appears as Sutta 118 of the Majjhima Nikāya (Ñanamoli & Bodhi, 2009). See bibliography for full reference.

3. From the Dhammapada (Buddharakkhita 1986). See bibliography for full reference.

4. For a fuller discussion of this topic, see our letter published in *The Psychologist*: W. Van Gordon and M. D. Griffiths, "For the Mindful Teaching of Mindfulness," *The Psychologist* 28 (2015): 514–19. Available at: https://thepsychologist.bps.org.uk/volume-28/july-2015/mindful-teaching-mindfulness.

6. A STICKY MIND

1. From the Dhammapada (Buddharakkhita 1986). See bibliography for full reference.

2. Game Transfer Phenomena was identified by Dr Angelica Ortiz de Gortari while she was conducting research at Nottingham Trent University, UK.

7. THE COMPASSIONATE HEART

1. See E. Shonin, W. Van Gordon, A. Compare, M. Zangeneh, and M. D. Griffiths, "Buddhist-Derived Loving-Kindness and Compassion Meditation for the Treatment of Psychopathology: A Systematic Review," *Mindfulness* 6 (2015): 1161–80.

2. We have used Buddharakkhita's (1986) version of the Dhammapada. See bibliography for full reference.

3. The full findings of the research study are reported in E. Shonin, W. Van Gordon, T. Dunn, N. Singh, N., and M. D. Griffiths, "Meditation Awareness Training for Work-Related Wellbeing and Job Performance: A Randomized Controlled Trial," *International Journal of Mental Health and Addiction* 12 (014): 806–23.

9. MINDFULNESS OF BIRTH, MINDFULNESS OF DEATH

1. From the Bhaddekaratta Sutta (Sutta 131 of the Majjhima Nikāya).

10. THE EMPTY SELF

1. The original version of the "Dream or Reality?" professor-student dialogue was published in *Philosophy Now*. E. Shonin and W. Van Gordon, "Dream or Reality?" *Philosophy Now*, 103 (2014): 54.

2. See A. D. M. Hofheinz, M, Ansmann, R. C. Bialczak, M. Lenander, E Lucero, . . . and A. N. Cleland, "Quantum Ground State and Single-Phonon Control of a Mechanical Resonator," *Nature*, 464 (2010): 697–703.

11. THE MINDFUL WARRIOR'S LINEAGE

1. The quote is from B. Ñanamoli and B. Bodhi, trans., *Sandaka Sutta* in *Majjhima Nikāya*, p. 624. See bibliography for full reference.

2. Gampopa, *The Jewel Ornament of Liberation: The Wish-Fulfilling Gem of the Noble Teachings*, ed. A. K. Trinlay Chodron, trans. K. Konchong Gyaltsen (New York: Snow Lion Publications, 1998), 331.

INDEX

ABOUT THE AUTHORS

William Van Gordon, PhD, is currently associate professor of contemplative psychology at the University of Derby, UK. He is widely regarded as a leading international expert in contemplative psychology and in the last five years alone, in addition to three books, William has published over one hundred academic papers, including in some of the world's leading psychology and medical journals. William's research has been described as "groundbreaking" by Grazia UK, and is regularly featured in the national TV, radio, and print media, with recent examples including the *BBC*, *ITV*, the *Times*, the *Telegraph*, the *Sun, Express, Metro, talkRadio, Mail Online, BBC Mundo*, and the *Bangkok Post*. William also writes a regular blog on contemplative psychology for *Psychology Today*. Prior to joining academia, William was a Buddhist monk for ten years and he has previously worked in senior management roles for Marconi Plc, PepsiCo International, and Aldi Stores Ltd. In the case of this latter position, he had total operational responsibility for a £28 million portfolio of six supermarkets with over sixty employees. William regularly travels all over the world to give keynote speeches, lectures, and workshops on meditation and contemplative practice

Edo Shonin, PhD, is a psychologist and was a Buddhist monk for thirty years. He helps to govern the Awake to Wisdom Centre for Meditation and Mindfulness Research. In line with his view that there are core practice and theoretical principles that unify all authentic Buddhist traditions, he received monastic ordinations in different Buddhist schools, including the higher ordination within the Theravada Buddhist tradition. He sits on the editorial board for numerous academic journals including *Mindfulness, Mindfulness and Compassion,* and the *International Journal of Mental Health and Addiction.* Edo is internationally recognized as a leading authority in the research and practice of Buddhist meditation. He has over one hundred academic publications relating to mindfulness and Buddhist meditation, including in some of the world's leading refereed medical and psychology journals. Edo is coeditor of two academic volumes published by Springer Publications: (i) *Mindfulness and Buddhist-Derived Approaches in Mental Health and Addiction,* and (ii) *The Buddhist Foundations of Mindfulness.* He regularly receives invitations to give keynote speeches, lectures, retreats, and workshops at a range of academic and nonacademic venues all over the world.

www.ingramcontent.com/pod-product-compliance
Lightning Source LLC
Chambersburg PA
CBHW030920150426
42812CB00046B/404